∾ S P U R G E O N ∾

Spiritual Warfare in a Believer's Life

∾∾

CHRISTIAN ∾ LIVING CLASSICS

CHRISTIAN LIVING CLASSICS
FROM EMERALD BOOKS

CHARLES SPURGEON: BELIEVER'S LIFE SERIES

Grace Abounding in a Believer's Life
A Passion for Holiness in a Believer's Life
The Power of Prayer in a Believer's Life
Spiritual Warfare in a Believer's Life
The Triumph of Faith in a Believer's Life
What the Holy Spirit Does in a Believer's Life

CHARLES SPURGEON: LIFE OF CHRIST SERIES

The Power of Christ's Miracles
The Power of Christ's Prayer Life
The Power of Christ's Second Coming
The Power of Christ's Tears
The Power of Christ the Warrior
The Power of the Cross of Christ

F. B. MEYER: BIBLE CHARACTER SERIES

The Life of Abraham: The Obedience of Faith
The Life of David: Shepherd, Psalmist, King
The Life of Joseph: Beloved, Hated, Exalted
The Life of Moses: The Servant of God
The Life of Paul: A Servant of Jesus Christ
The Life of Peter: Fisherman, Disciple, Apostle

30-DAY DEVOTIONAL TREASURIES

Charles Finney on Spiritual Power
George Müller on Faith
Andrew Murray on Holiness
Hudson Taylor on Spiritual Secrets
Charles Spurgeon on Prayer
R. A. Torrey on the Holy Spirit

IN HIS PRESENCE: DAILY DEVOTIONALS (full year)

CHARLES SPURGEON
~ Christian Living Classics ~

Spiritual Warfare in a Believer's Life

~ Compiled and Edited by ROBERT HALL ~

Emerald Books

P.O. Box 635 • Lynnwood, Washington 98046

Scripture quotations are taken from the King James Version of the Bible.

ISBN 1-883002-02-8

Published by Emerald Books
P.O. box 635
Lynnwood, Washington 98046

Printed in the United States of America

To My Son

Nils

"I write to you, young men, because you are
strong, and the word of God abides in you, and
you have overcome the evil one."

About the Editor

ROBERT HALL is the pseudonym for Lance Wubbels, the managing editor of Bethany House Publishers. His interest in the writings of Charles Spurgeon began while doing research on an editorial project that required extensive reading of Spurgeon's sermons. He discovered a wealth of sermon classics that are filled with practical, biblical insight for every believer and written in a timeless manner that makes them as relevant today as the day they were spoken. His desire is to select and present Spurgeon's writings in a way that will appeal to a wide audience of readers and allow one of the greatest preachers of all time to enrich believers' lives.

About the Author

CHARLES HADDON SPURGEON (1834–1892) was the remarkable British "Boy Preacher of the Fens" who became one of the truly greatest preachers of all time. Coming from a flourishing country pastorate in 1854, he accepted a call to pastor London's New Park Street Chapel. This building soon proved too small and so work on Spurgeon's Metropolitan Tabernacle was begun in 1859. Meanwhile his weekly sermons were being printed and having a remarkable sale—25,000 copies every week in 1865 and translated into more than twenty languages.

Spurgeon built the Metropolitan Tabernacle into a congregation of over 6,000 and added well over 14,000 members during his thirty-eight-year London ministry. The combination of his clear voice, his mastery of language, his sure grasp of Scripture, and a deep love for Christ produced some of the noblest preaching of any age. An astounding 3,561 sermons have been preserved in sixty-three volumes, *The New Park Street Pulpit* and *The Metropolitan Tabernacle Pulpit*, from which the chapters of this book have been selected and edited.

During his lifetime, Spurgeon is estimated to have preached to 10,000,000 people. He remains history's most widely read preacher. There is more available material written by Spurgeon than by any other Christian author, living or dead. His sixty-three volumes of sermons stand as the largest set of books by a single author in the history of Christianity, comprising the equivalent to the twenty-seven volumes of the ninth edition of the *Encyclopedia Britannica*.

Contents

Introduction

WHEN CHARLES SPURGEON ARRIVED at The New Park Street Chapel in 1854, the congregation had 232 members. By the end of his pastorate, that number had officially increased to 5,311 members, making it the largest independent congregation in the world. No building seemed big enough to house all those that wanted to hear him preach. Occasionally Spurgeon asked members of his congregation not to attend the next Sunday's service so that newcomers might find a seat. During one 1879 service, the regular congregation left so that newcomers waiting outside might get in, and the building immediately filled again. He once addressed an audience of 23,654 people without a microphone or any mechancial amplification.

What was it about his preaching that drew in multitudes from all levels of British society? Why would Prime Minister W.E. Gladstone, members of the royal family, and members of Parliament attend his church when it had become known as a "church of shopkeepers"? Undoubtedly, the combination of a beautiful speaking voice, a dramatic flair and style that was captivating, a profound depth and breadth of spirituality, as well as a powerful commitment to a biblical theology go a long way to explaining how he took the city of London by storm. But perhaps the most signficant factor was that Spurgeon always strove to be a communicator. He preached to the common people in their own language and in a way that was criticized as "vulgar." He addressed people where they were and spoke simply to their deepest needs. He painted word pictures in a dramatic, eloquent, even humorous way. In a word, he was a passionate biblical expositor of the gospel who made his message culturally relevant.

Judging from the large number of Spurgeon sermons that were specifically directed to the subject of spiritual warfare, one gets the clear impression that this was an area of significant concern for the common people of his day. Many of his sermons were titled by such themes as "Christ the Conqueror of Satan," "An Antidote to Satan's Devices," "Satanic Hindrances," and the Christian armor. But in keeping with his practical style, there is nothing abstract, ethereal, or mystical about Spurgeon's approach. He directed his focus where he saw Satan at work in the lives of people—enslaving them in sin, keeping them from the influence of the gospel, hindering their spiritual development, preventing the gospel from having its full influence, bringing discouragement, depression, and moral failure.

Against that backdrop, Spurgeon preached the mighty victory of Christ over Satan and his powers of darkness. The cross and the resurrection stand as the battleground where Christ championed the public defeat of mankind's enemy and the reclaiming of all that was lost by the Fall. Believers share that victory in their union with Christ—a victory that not only protects them on their journey to heaven but a victory that makes them more than conquerors during their lifetimes. Armed with the Word of God and the Christian graces, believers have the power to stand in battle as well as take the enemy's ground. And it's a victory that makes a difference where believers live—in the home, in the work place, and especially in the privacy of the Christian life where besetting sins, satanic lies, and spiritual attack have taken their toll.

Spurgeon's message was born out of his own personal experience. Before his conversion, he was spiritually tormented for five years with the horror of his lostness and never stopped preaching about the deliverance Christ brings to weary souls. During his years of ministry, he was slandered and scorned both in the press and by other ministers. Spurgeon took seriously the awesome responsibility of the spiritual care of so large a congregation, laboring long and hard in the ministry. He suffered emotionally and was well acquainted with recurring depression and doubt. And he was seldom free from physical pain from 1871 on—suffering from gout and often afflicted for weeks and even months at a time. He was a seasoned veteran in meeting Satan at every corner and defeating Satan in the power of the gospel.

I invite you to read these twelve powerful chapters on spiritual warfare as you would listen to a trusted and skilled pastor. There is nothing speculative about Spurgeon's teaching; nothing that will leave you in the heavenly places wondering about the principalities and powers and how you are to engage them. Spurgeon will meet you where you live in an understandable manner that inspires and challenges. Life-changing messages on spiritual victory await you.

Careful editing has helped to sharpen the focus of these sermons while retaining the authentic and timeless flavor they undoubtedly bring.

Who are those grim monsters at the Conqueror's chariot's wheels? First of all there is the archenemy. Look to the old serpent, bound and fettered; how he writhes his ragged length along! His azure hues all tarnished with trailing in the dust, his scales despoiled of their once vaunted brightness. Now is captivity led captive, and death and hell shall be cast into the lake of fire. With what derision is the chief of rebels regarded. How he has become the object of everlasting contempt! "He that sitteth in the heavens shall laugh: the Lord shall have them in derision" (Ps. 2:4). Behold how the serpent's head is broken and the dragon is trampled under foot. And now regard attentively the hideous monster, Sin, chained hand in hand with his satanic sire. See how he rolls his fiery eyeballs; mark how he twists and writhes in agonies. Mark how he glares upon the holy city but is unable to spit his venom there, for he is chained and gagged and dragged along an unwilling captive at the wheels of the victor. And there, too, is old Death—the grim king of terrors—with his darts all broken and his hands behind him, for he too is a captive. Hark to the songs of the redeemed, of those who have entered into Paradise, as they see these mighty prisoners dragged along! "Worthy is He," they shout, "to live and reign at His Almighty Father's side, for He hath ascended up on high."

Chapter One

Christ Triumphant

And having spoiled principalities and powers, he made a show of them openly, triumphing over them in it—Colossians 2:15.

TO THE EYE OF REASON, the cross is the center of sorrow and the lowest depth of shame. Jesus dies a criminal's death. He hangs upon the cross of a felon and pours out His blood upon the common mount of doom with thieves for His companions. In the midst of mockery, jest, scorn, and blasphemy, He gives up the ghost. Earth rejects Him and lifts Him from her surface, and heaven affords Him no light but darkens the midday sun in the hour of His extremity. Deeper in woe than the Savior dived, imagination cannot descend. Satanic malice itself could not invent a blacker calumny than was cast on Him. Jesus hid not His face from shame and spitting, and what shame and spitting it was! To the world, the cross must ever be the emblem of shame: to the Jew a stumbling block and to the Greek foolishness.

How different, however, is the view that presents itself to the eye of faith. Faith knows no shame in the cross except the shame of those who nailed the Savior there; it sees no ground for scorn, but it hurls indignant scorn at sin, the enemy that pierced the Lord. Faith sees woe, indeed; but from this woe, it marks a fount of mercy springing. It is true it mourns a dying Savior, but it beholds

Him bringing life and immortality to light at the very moment when His soul was eclipsed in the shadow of death. Faith regards the cross, not as the emblem of shame but as the token of glory. The sons of Belial lay the cross in the dust, but the Christian makes a constellation of it and sees it glittering in the seventh heaven. Man spits upon it, but believers, having angels for their companions, bow down and worship Him who ever lives though once was slain.

Our opening text presents us with a portion of the view that faith is certain to discover when its eyes are anointed with the eye salve of the Holy Spirit. It tells us that the cross was Jesus Christ's field of triumph. There He fought, and there He conquered. As a victor on the cross, He divided the spoil. Nay, more than this: in our text, the cross is spoken of as being Christ's triumphal chariot in which He rode when He led captivity captive and received gifts for men. Calvin thus admirably expounds the last sentence of the text:

> The expression in the Greek allows, it is true, of our reading— *in Himself;* the connection of the passage, however, requires that we read it otherwise; for what would be meager as applied to Christ, suits admirably well as applied to the cross. For as He had previously compared the cross to a signal trophy or show of triumph, in which Christ led about His enemies, so He now also compares it to a triumphal car in which He showed Himself in great magnificence. For there is no tribunal so magnificent, no throne so stately, no show of triumph so distinguished, no chariot so elevated, as is the gibbet on which Christ has subdued death and the devil, the prince of death; nay, more, has utterly trodden them under His feet.

My purpose is first to describe *Christ as defeating His enemies on the cross.* Having done that, I shall lead your imagination and faith farther on to see *the Savior in triumphal procession upon His cross,* leading His enemies captive and making a show of them openly before the eyes of the astonished universe.

Christ Defeating the Principalities and Powers

Satan, leagued with sin and death, had made this world the home of woe. The Prince of the power of the air, not content with his dominions in hell, must invade this fair earth. He found our first parents in the midst of Eden; he tempted them to forego their allegiance to the King of heaven; and they became at once his bondslaves—bondslaves forever, had the Lord of heaven not interposed to ransom them. The voice of mercy was heard while the fetters were being riveted upon their feet, crying, *"You shall yet be free!"* In the fullness of time, there shall come One who shall bruise the serpent's head and deliver His prisoners from the house of bondage. Long did the promise tarry. The earth groaned and travailed in its bondage. Man was Satan's slave, and heavy were the clanking chains that were upon his soul.

At last, in the fullness of time, the Deliverer came forth, born of a woman. This infant Conqueror lay in the manger—*He* who was one day to bind the old dragon and cast him into the bottomless pit. When the old serpent knew that his enemy was born, he conspired to put Him to death; he leagued with Herod to destroy the young child, but the providence of God preserved the future Conqueror. When the Deliverer had come to fullness of years, He made His public advent and began to preach liberty to the captives and the opening of the prison to them who were bound. Then Satan again shot forth his arrows and sought to end the existence of the woman's seed. By diverse means, he sought to slay Him before His time. The Jews took up stones to stone Him; they sought to cast Him headlong down from the brow of a hill. Dangers might surround Him, but He was invulnerable till the time was come.

At last the tremendous day arrived. Foot to foot, the Conqueror must fight with the dread tyrant. A voice was heard in heaven: "This is your hour, and the power of darkness." And Christ Himself exclaimed, "Now is the crisis of this world; now must the prince of darkness be cast out." From the table of communion, the Redeemer arose at midnight and marched forth to battle. How dreadful was the contest! In the very first onset, the mighty Conqueror seemed Himself to be vanquished. Beaten to the earth at the first assault, He fell upon His knees and cried, "My father, if it be possible let this cup pass from Me." Revived in strength, made strong by heaven, from this hour never did He utter a word that looked like renouncing the fight. From the terrible skirmish all red with bloody sweat, He dashed into the thick of the battle. The kiss of Judas was, as it were, the first sounding of the trumpet; Pilate's tribunal was the glittering of the spear; the cruel lash was the crossing of the swords. But the cross was the center of the battle; there on the top of Calvary must the dread fight of eternity be fought. Now must the Son of God arise and gird His sword upon His thigh. Dread defeat or glorious conquest awaits the Champion of the church. Which shall it be?

We hold our breath with anxious suspense while the storm is raging. I hear the trumpet sound. The howlings and yells of hell rise in awful clamor. The pit is emptying out its legions. Terrible as lions, hungry as wolves, and black as night, the demons rush on in myriads. Satan's reserved forces—those who had long been kept against this day of terrible battle—are roaring from their dens. See how countless are their armies and how fierce their countenances. Brandishing his sword, the archfiend leads the van, bidding his followers fight neither with small nor with great, save only with the King of Israel. Terrible are the leaders of the battle. Sin is there, and all its innumerable offspring, spitting forth the venom of asps and fastening their poison fangs in the Savior's flesh. Death is there upon his pale horse, and his cruel dart rends its way through the body of Jesus even to His inmost heart. He is "exceeding sorrowful, even unto death." Hell comes, with all its burning coals and fiery darts.

Chief and head among them is Satan. Remembering well the ancient day when Christ hurled him from the battlements of heaven, he rushes with all his malice yelling to the attack. The darts shot into the air are so countless that they blind the sun. Darkness covers the battlefield, and like that of Egypt, it was a darkness that was felt. Long does the battle seem to waver, for there is but one against many. One man—nay, tell it, lest any should misunderstand me—one *God* stands in battle array against ten thousand of principalities and powers. On, on they come, and He receives them all. Silently at first He permits their ranks to break upon Him, too terrible enduring hardness to spare a thought for shouting.

At last the battle cry is heard. He who is fighting for His people begins to shout, but it is a shout that makes the church tremble. He cries, "I thirst!" The battle is so hot upon Him and the dust so thick that He is choked with thirst. He cries, "I thirst!" Surely, now, He is about to be defeated. But wait; the enemy is but rushing to His destruction. In vain their fury and rage—for see the last rank is charging—the battle of ages is almost over. At last the darkness is dispersed. Hark how the Conqueror cries, "It is finished!" And where are His enemies now? They are all dead. There lies the king of terrors, pierced through with one of his own darts! There lies Satan with his head all bleeding, broken! Yonder crawls the broken-backed serpent, writhing in ghastly misery! As for sin, it is cut in pieces and scattered to the winds of heaven! "*It is finished!*" cries the Conqueror. "I have trodden the winepress alone; . . . I [have trampled] them in my fury; and their blood [is] sprinkled upon my garments" (Isa. 63:3).

And now He proceeds to *divide the spoil.*

We pause to remark that when the spoil is divided, it is a sure token that the battle is completely won. The enemy will never allow the spoil to be divided among the conquerors as long as he has any strength remaining. We may gather from our text that Jesus Christ has totally routed, thoroughly defeated once for all, and put to retreat all His enemies.

What does this expression of Christ dividing the spoil mean? I take it that it means, first of all, that *Christ disarmed all His enemies.* Satan came against Christ; he had in his hand a sharp sword called the Law, dipped in the poison of sin, so that every wound that the law inflicted was deadly. Christ dashed this sword out of Satan's hand, and there stood the prince of darkness unarmed. His helmet was cleft in two, and his head was crushed as with a rod of iron. Death rose against Christ. The Savior snatched Death's quiver from him, emptied out all his darts, broke them in two, gave Death back the feather end but kept the poisoned barbs from him, that he might never destroy the ransomed. Sin came against Christ, but sin was utterly cut in pieces. It had been Satan's armorbearer, but its shield was cast away and lay dead upon the plain.

What a remarkable picture to behold all the enemies of Christ totally disarmed. Satan has nothing left now with which he may attack us. He may attempt to injure us, but wound us he never can, for his sword and spear are utterly taken away. In the old battles, especially among the Romans, after the enemy had been overcome, it was the custom to take away all their weapons and ammunition. Afterward they were stripped of their armor and garments, their hands were tied behind their backs, and they were made to pass under the yoke. Now, even so has Christ defeated sin, death, and hell. He has made them all to pass under the yoke, so that now they are our slaves, and we in Christ are conquerors of them.

I take it this is the first meaning of dividing the spoil—total disarming of the adversary.

When the victors divide the spoil, they carry away all the treasures that belong to their enemies. They dismantle their fortresses and ransack their stores so that in the future they may not be able to renew the attack. Christ has done this with all His enemies. Old Satan had taken from us all our possessions. Paradise Satan had added to his territories. All the joy and happiness and peace of man Satan had taken—not that he could enjoy them himself, but that he delighted to thrust us down into poverty and damnation. Now, all our lost inheritances Christ has gotten back to us. Paradise is ours, and more than all the joy and happiness that Adam had, Christ has brought back to us. O robber of our race, how you are spoiled and carried away captive! Did you despoil Adam of his riches? The second Adam has rent them from you! How the hammer of the whole earth is cut asunder and broken and the waster is become desolate. Once again the meek shall inherit the earth. "Then is the prey of a great spoil divided, the lame take the prey."

Moreover, when victors divide the spoil, it is usual to take away all the ornaments—the crowns and the jewels—from the enemy. Christ on the cross did the like with Satan. Satan had a haughty crown of triumph on his head. "I overcame the first Adam," he said. Christ snatched the crown from Satan's brow in the hour when He bruised the serpent's head. And now Satan cannot boast of a single victory; he is thoroughly defeated. In the first skirmish, he vanquished manhood, but in the second battle, manhood vanquished him. Satan is no longer the prince of God's people. His reigning power is gone. He may tempt, but he cannot compel. He may threaten, but he cannot subdue, for the crown is taken from his head, and the mighty are brought low. O sing unto the Lord a new song, all His people; make a joyful noise unto Him with psalms, all His redeemed, for He has broken in sunder the gates of brass and cut the bars of iron; He has broken the bow and cut the spear in sunder; He has burned the chariots in the fire; He has dashed in pieces our enemies and divided the spoil with the strong.

How does this apply to us? Simply this. If Christ on the cross has spoiled Satan, let us not be afraid to encounter this great enemy of our souls. In all things we must be made like Christ. We must bear our cross, and on that cross we must fight as Christ did with sin and death and hell. Let us not fear. The result of the battle is certain, for as the Lord our Savior has overcome once, even so shall we most surely conquer in Him.

Never be afraid when the evil one comes upon you. If he accuses you, reply to him: "Who shall lay anything to the charge of God's elect?" If he condemns you, laugh him to scorn, crying: "Who is he that condemneth? It is Christ that died, yea rather hath risen again." If he threatens to divide you from Christ's love, encounter him with confidence: "I am persuaded that neither things present nor things to come, nor height nor depth, nor any other creature shall be able to separate us from the love of God that is in Christ Jesus our Lord." If he lets loose your sins upon you, dash the hell-dogs aside with this: "If any man sin, *we* have an advocate with the Father, Jesus Christ the righteous." If death should threaten you, shout in his very face: "O death! where is thy sting; O grave! where is thy victory."

Hold up the cross before you. Let that be your shield and buckler, and rest assured that as your Master not only routed the foe but afterward took the spoil, it shall be so with you. Your battles with Satan will turn to your advantage. The more numerous the attacks, the greater shall be your share of the spoil. Your tribulation shall work patience, and your patience experience, and your experience hope—a hope that does not disappoint. Put yourself in array against sin and Satan. All you who bend the bow, shoot at them; spare no arrows, for your enemies are rebels against God. Go up against them, put your feet upon their necks, fear not, neither be dismayed, for the battle is the Lord's, and the Lord will deliver your enemies into your hands.

Be very courageous, remembering that you have to fight with a stingless dragon. He may hiss, but his teeth are broken and his poison fang extracted. You have to do battle with an enemy already scarred by your Master's weapons. Every blow you give him takes it toll upon him, for he has nothing to protect him. Christ stripped him naked, divided his armor, and left him defenseless. The enemy may rush in upon you with hideous noise and terrible alarms, but there is no real cause for fear. Stand fast in the Lord. Rejoice in the day of battle, for it is for you but the beginning of an eternity of triumph.

The Triumph

When a Roman general had performed great feats in a foreign country, his highest reward was that the senate decree him a triumph. Of course, there was a division of spoil made on the battlefield, and each soldier and captain took his share, but every man looked forward rapturously to the day when they should enjoy the public triumph. On a certain set day, the gates of Rome were thrown open, the houses were all decorated with ornaments, the people climbed to the tops of the houses or stood in great crowds along the streets. The gates were opened, and the first legion began to stream in with its banners flying and its trumpets sounding. The people saw the stern warriors as they marched along the street returning from their blood-red fields of battle.

After one half of the army had entered, your eye would rest upon one who was the center of attraction: riding in a noble chariot drawn by white horses, there came the conqueror himself, crowned with the laurel crown and standing erect. Chained to his chariot were the kings and mighty men of the regions whom he had conquered. Immediately behind them came part of the booty. There were carried the ivory and the ebony and the beasts of the different countries that he had subdued. After these came the rest of the soldiers, a long, long stream of valiant men, all of them sharing the triumphs of their captain. Behind them came banners, the old flags that had floated aloft in the battle, the standards that had been taken from the enemy. After these, large painted emblems of the great victories of the warrior. Upon one there would be a huge map depicting the rivers that he had crossed or the seas through which his navy had found their way. Everything was represented in a picture, and the populace gave a fresh shout as they saw the memorial of each triumph. And then would come the prisoners of less eminent rank. Then the rear would be closed with the sound of trumpet, adding to the acclamation of the throng. It was a noble day for old Rome. Children would never forget those triumphs; they would estimate their years from the time of one triumph to another. High holiday was kept. Women cast down flowers before the true monarch of the day.

The Apostle Paul takes this as a representation of what Christ did on the cross. He says, "Jesus made a show of them openly, triumphing over them in it." Have you ever thought that the cross could be the scene of a triumph? Most of the old commentators can hardly conceive it to be true. They say, "This must certainly refer to Christ's resurrection and ascension." Nevertheless, the Scripture says that even on the cross, Christ enjoyed a triumph. Yes, while those hands were bleeding, the acclamations of angels were being poured upon His head. Yes, while those feet were being rent with the nails, the noblest spirits in the world were crowding round Him with admiration. And when upon that blood-stained cross He died in agonies unutterable, there was heard a shout such as never was heard before the ransomed in heaven, and all the angels of God with loudest harmony chanted His praise. Then was sung, in fullest chorus, the song of Moses—the servant of God and of the Lamb—for He had sorely wounded the dragon.

The cross is the ground of Christ's ultimate triumph. Christ may be said to have really triumphed there because it was by that one act of His—that one offering of Himself—that He completely vanquished all His foes and forever sat down at the right hand of the Majesty in the heavens. In the cross, to the spiritual eye, every victory of Christ is contained: the germ of Christ's glories may be discovered by the eye of faith in the agonies of the cross. Bear with me while I humbly attempt to depict the triumph that now results from the cross.

Christ has forever overcome all His foes and divided the spoil upon the battlefield, and now He is enjoying the well-earned reward and triumph of His fearful struggle. Lift up your eyes to the battlements of heaven, the great metropolis of God. The pearly gates are wide open, and the city shines with her bejeweled walls like a bride prepared for her husband. Do you see the angels crowding to the battlements? Do you observe them on every mansion of the celestial city, eagerly looking for something that has not arrived?

At last, there is heard the sound of a trumpet, and the angels hurry to the gates; the vanguard of the redeemed is approaching the city. Abel comes in alone, clothed in crimson garb, the herald of a glorious army of martyrs. Hark to the shout of acclamation! This is the first of Christ's warriors—at once a soldier and a trophy—who have been delivered. Close at his heels there follow others, who in those early times had learned of the coming Savior's fame. Behind them a mighty host may be discovered of patriarchal veterans who have witnessed to the coming of the Lord. See Enoch still walking with his God and singing sweetly, "Behold, the Lord cometh with ten thousands of his saints" (Jude 14). There, too, is Noah, who had sailed in the ark with the Lord as his pilot. Then follow Abraham, Isaac, and Jacob, Moses, Joshua, Samuel, and David—all mighty men of valor. Hearken to them as they enter! Every one of them, waving his helmet in the air, cries, "Unto him that loved us, and washed us from our sins in his own blood . . . to him be glory and dominion for ever and ever" (Rev. 1:5–6).

Look with admiration upon this noble army! Mark the heroes as they march along the golden streets, everywhere meeting an enthusiastic welcome from the angels who have kept their first estate. On, on they pour, those countless legions—was there ever such a sight? It is not the pageant of a day, but the "show" of all time. For four thousand years on streams the army of Christ's redeemed. Sometimes there is a short rank, for the people have been often diminished and brought low. But then a crowd succeeds, and on, on, still on they come, all shouting, all praising Him who loved them and gave Himself for them.

But see, *He* comes! I see His immediate herald, clad in a garment of camel's hair and a leather girdle about his loins. The Prince of the house of David is not far behind. Let every eye be open. Now mark how not only angels but also the redeemed crowd the windows of heaven! He comes! He comes! It is Christ Himself! Lash the snow-white coursers up the everlasting hills: "Lift up your heads, O ye gates; and be ye lifted up, ye everlasting doors; and the King of glory shall come in" (Ps. 24:7). See, He enters in the midst of acclamations. It is He! But He is not crowned with thorns. It is He! But though His hands wear the scar, they are stained with blood no longer. His eyes are as a flame of fire, and on His head are many crowns; and He has on His vesture and on His thigh written, KING OF KINGS AND LORD OF LORDS. Clothed in a vesture dipped in blood, He stands confessed the emperor of heaven and earth.

On, on He rides, and louder than the noise of many waters and like great thunders are the acclamations that surround Him! See how John's vision becomes a reality, for now we can see for ourselves and hear with our ears the new song whereof he writes:

> And they sung a new song, saying, Thou art worthy to take the book, and to open the seals thereof: for thou was slain, and hast redeemed us to God by thy blood out of every kindred, and tongue, and people, and nation; and hast made us unto our God kings and priests: and we shall reign on the earth. And I beheld, and I heard the voice of many angels round about the throne and the beasts and the elders: and the number of them was ten thousand times ten thousand, and thousands of thousands; saying with a loud voice, Worthy is the Lamb that was slain to receive power, and riches, and wisdom, and strength, and honour, and glory, and blessing" (Rev. 5:9–12).

But who are those at His chariot's wheels? Who are those grim monsters that come howling in the rear? I know them. First of all there is the archenemy. Look to the old serpent, bound and fettered; how he writhes his ragged length along! His azure hues all tarnished with trailing in the dust, his scales despoiled of their once vaunted brightness. Now is captivity led captive, and death and hell shall be cast into the lake of fire. With what derision is the chief of rebels regarded. How he has become the object of everlasting contempt! "He that sitteth in the heavens shall laugh: the Lord shall have them in derision" (Ps. 2:4). Behold how the serpent's head is broken and the dragon is trampled under foot. And now regard attentively the hideous monster, *Sin*, chained hand in hand with his satanic sire. See how he rolls his fiery eyeballs; mark how he twists and writhes in agonies. Mark how he glares upon the holy city but is unable to spit his venom there, for he is chained and gagged and dragged along an unwilling captive at the wheels of the victor. And there, too, is old Death—the grim king of terrors—with his darts all broken and his hands behind him, for he too is a captive. Hark to the songs of the redeemed, of those who have entered into Paradise, as they see these mighty prisoners dragged along! "Worthy is He," they shout, "to live and reign at His Almighty Father's side, for He hath ascended up on high; He hath led captivity captive and received gifts for men."

And now behind Him I see the great mass of His people streaming in. The apostles arrive first in one group hymning their Lord, and then their immediate successors, and then a long array of those who through cruel mockings and blood, through flame and sword, have followed their Master. These are those of whom the world was not worthy, brightest among the stars of heaven. Regard also the mighty preachers and confessors of the faith—Chrysostom, Athanasius, Augustine, and the like. Witness their holy unanimity in praising their Lord. Then let your eye run along the glittering ranks till you come to the days of the Reformation. I see in the midst of the squadron, Luther, Calvin, and Zwingli, three holy brothers. I see just before them Wycliffe, Huss, and Jerome of Prague, all marching together. And then I see a number that no man can number who now follow in the rear of the King of kings and Lord of lords. And looking down to our own time I see the stream broader and wider. For many are the soldiers who have in those days entered into their Master's triumph. We may mourn their absence from *us*, but we must rejoice in their presence with the *Lord*.

But what is the unanimous shout, what is the one song that still rolls from the first rank to the last? It is this: "Unto him that loved us, and washed us from our sins in his own blood, . . . to him be glory and dominion forever and ever" (Rev. 1:5–6). Have they changed the tune? Have they put the crown on another head or elevated another hero into the chariot? Ah, no. They are content still to let the triumphant procession stream along its glorious length, still to rejoice as they behold fresh trophies of His love, for every soldier is a trophy, every warrior in Christ's army is another proof of His power to save and His victory over death and hell.

I cannot now describe the mighty pictures at the end of the procession: the towns He had taken, the rivers He had passed, the provinces He had subdued, the battles He had fought. I might present to you first of all the picture of hell's dungeons blown to atoms. Satan had prepared deep in the depths of darkness a prison for God's elect, but Christ has not left one stone upon another. On the picture I see the chains broken in pieces, the prison doors burned with fire, and all the depths shaken to their foundations. On another picture I see heaven open to all believers; I see the gates that were tightly shut heaved open by the golden lever of Christ's atonement. I see on another picture the grave despoiled; I behold Jesus in it, slumbering for a while and then rolling away the stone and rising to immortality and glory. But we cannot stay to describe these mighty pictures of the victories of His love. We know that the time shall come when the triumphant procession shall cease, when the last of His redeemed shall have entered into the city of happiness and joy, and when, with the shout of a trumpet heard for the last time, He shall ascend to heaven and take His people up to reign with God, even our Father, forever and ever, world without end.

Will you be there—will you see this pomp? Will you behold His final triumph over sin, death, and hell? Do you believe in the Lord Jesus Christ? Is He your confidence and trust? Have you committed your soul to His keeping? If you can answer yes, your eyes shall see Him in the day of His glory; nay, you shall share His glory and sit with Him upon His throne, even as He has overcome and sits down with His Father upon His throne. May God enlarge your faith and strengthen your hope and inflame your love and make you ready to be made partakers of the inheritance of the saints in light, that when He shall come with flying clouds on wings of wind, you may be ready to meet Him and may with Him ascend to gaze forever on the vision of His glory.

*A*bove all, if we would successfully resist Satan, we must look not merely to revealed wisdom but to Incarnate Wisdom. Here must be the chief place of resort for every tempted soul! We must flee to Him "who of God is made unto us wisdom, and righteousness, and sanctification, and redemption" (1 Cor. 1:30). He must teach us, He must guide us, He must be our All-in-all. We must keep close to Him in communion. The sheep are never so safe from the wolf as when they are near the shepherd. We shall never be so secure from the arrows of Satan as when we have our head lying on the Savior's bosom. Believer, walk according to His example, live daily in His fellowship, trust always in His blood, and in this way you shall be more than a conqueror over the subtlety and craft of Satan himself.

Chapter Two

An Antidote to Satan's Devices

Now the serpent was more subtle than any beast of the field which the LORD God had made—Genesis 3:1.

"THAT OLD SERPENT," called the devil, Satan, deceiver, or liar, is the one of whom our Lord Jesus said to the Jews, "When he speaketh a lie, he speaketh of his own: for he is a liar, and the father of it" (John 8:44). God was pleased in creation to give to many beasts subtlety—to some, cunning combined with strength, and to others, instincts of most marvelous wisdom—for self-preservation and the procuring of food. But all the wise instincts and subtlety of the beasts of the field are far excelled by the subtlety of Satan. Even man, though far more cunning than any mere creature, is no match for the cunning of Satan.

Satan is the master deceiver and is able to overcome us for several reasons. A primary reason that Satan should be cunning is that he is *malicious*, for malice is of all things the most productive of cunning. When a man is revengeful, it is amazing how cunning he is to find opportunities to strike out. When enmity thoroughly possesses his soul and pours its venom into his very blood, he will become exceedingly crafty in the means he uses to provoke and injure his adversary. No, there is no one more full of malice against man than Satan, as he proves every day, and that malice sharpens his inherent wisdom so that he becomes exceedingly subtle.

Besides, Satan is *an angel*, though a fallen one. We doubt not, from certain hints in Scripture, that he occupied a very high place in the hierarchy of angels before he fell, and we know that those mighty beings are endowed with vast intellectual powers far surpassing any given to mankind. Therefore, we must not expect that a man, unaided from above, should ever be a match for an angel, especially an angel whose intellect has been sharpened by malice.

Satan may well be cunning now—I may truthfully say, more cunning than he was in the days of Adam—for *he has had long dealings with the human race*. His temptation of Eve was his first occasion of dealing with mankind, but he has long since exercised all his diabolical thought and mighty powers to annoy and ruin men. There is not a saint whom he has not beset and not a sinner whom he has not misled. Together with his troops of evil spirits, he has continually exercised a terrible control over the sons of men; he is therefore well skilled in all the arts of temptation.

Never has an anatomist so understood the human body as Satan does the human soul. Satan has not been "tempted in all points," but he has tempted others in all points. He has tried to assail our manhood from the crown of our head to the sole of our foot, and he has explored every outwork of our nature and even the most secret caverns of our soul. He has climbed into the citadel of our heart, and he has lived there; he has searched our heart's inmost recesses and dived into its profoundest depths. I suppose there is nothing of human nature that Satan cannot unravel. Though, doubtless, he is the biggest fool that has ever existed, yet beyond all doubt, he is the craftiest of fools. I may add, that is no great paradox, for craft is always folly and craftiness is but another shape of departure from wisdom.

First, I shall define *the craft and subtlety of Satan* and the methods in which Satan attacks our soul. Second, I shall give you a few words of admonition with regard to *the wisdom that we must exercise against Satan* and the only means that we can use effectually to prevent Satan's subtlety from being the instrument of our destruction.

The Craft and Subtlety of Satan

Satan reveals his craft and subtlety by *the methods of his attack.* He does not attack with unbelief and distrustfulness the man who is calm and at ease. Satan attacks such a man in a more vulnerable point than that. Self-love, self-confidence, worldliness—these will be the weapons that Satan will use against him. There is a person who is noted for depression and lack of mental vitality. It is not probable that Satan will try to puff such a person up with pride. Rather by examining him and discovering where his weak point is, Satan will tempt this person to doubt his calling and endeavor to drive him to despair. There is a man of robust physical health and vigorous mental powers who is enjoying the promises and delighting in the ways of God. Possibly Satan will not attack this man with unbelief, because he feels that such a man has armor for that particular point, but he will attack him with pride or some temptation to lust. Satan will most thoroughly and carefully examine us, and if he shall find us to be, like Achilles, vulnerable nowhere else but in our heel, he will shoot his arrows at our heel.

I believe that Satan seldom attacks a man in a place of strength, but he generally looks for the weak point, the besetting sin. "There," says he, "there will I strike the blow." God help us in the hour of battle and the time of conflict! Indeed, unless the Lord should help us, this crafty foe might easily find enough joints in our armor and soon send the deadly arrow into our soul, so that we should fall down wounded before him. And yet I have noticed, strangely enough, that Satan does sometimes tempt men with the very thing that you might suppose would never be a problem for them. What do you imagine was John Knox's last temptation upon his dying bed? Perhaps there was never a man who more fully understood than John Knox did the great doctrine that "by grace are ye saved." Knox thundered the doctrine from the pulpit and declared it boldly and bravely. But—will you believe it—that old enemy of souls attacked John Knox with self-righteousness on his death bed? He came to him and said, "How bravely you have served your Master, John! You have never quailed before the face of man; you have faced kings and princes, and yet you have never trembled; such a man as you are may walk into the kingdom of heaven on your own footing, and wear your own garment at the wedding of the Most High." Sharp and terrible was the struggle that John Knox had with the enemy of souls over that temptation.

I can describe a similar experience of my own. I thought within myself that of all the people in the world, I was the most free from care. It had never troubled my thoughts for a moment to care for the things of this world. I had always had all I needed, and I felt beyond the reach of anxiety about such matters. And yet, but a little while ago, a most frightful temptation overtook me, casting me into a worldliness of care and thought. Though I wrestled with all my might against the temptation, it was long before I could overcome these distrustful thoughts regarding God's providence. Yet I must confess, there was not the slightest reason, as far as I could see, why such thoughts should break in upon me. For that reason, and for many more, I hate the devil worse and worse every day, and I have vowed, if it is possible by preaching the Word of God, to seek to shake the very pillars of Satan's kingdom.

The modes of Satan's attack betray Satan's subtlety. While you are putting on your helmet, Satan is seeking to thrust his fiery sword into your heart; or while you are looking after your breast-plate, he is lifting up his battle-ax to split your skull; and while you are seeing to both helmet and breastplate, he is seeking to trip your foot. He is vigilant to see where you are not looking or when you are sleeping. Take heed to yourselves, therefore: "Put on the whole armour of God" (Eph. 6:11); "Be sober, be vigilant; because your adversary the devil, as a roaring lion, walketh about, seeking whom he may devour: whom resist stedfast in the faith" (1 Pet. 5:8–9); and God help you to prevail over him!

A second thing in which Satan discloses his cunning is *the weapons that he will often use against us.* Sometimes he will attack the child of God with past remembrances of the days of his carnal state, but far more frequently he will attack him with texts of Scripture. When he shoots his arrow against a believer, he often wings it with God's own Word. Like the eagle, when the arrow was drinking up his heart's blood, saw that the feather that winged it to his bosom had been plucked from his own breast, so the Christian will often have a similar experience. "Ah!" he will say, "here is a text that I love, taken from the Book that I prize, yet it is turned against me." Have you not found it so? Satan attacked

Christ with an "It is written," so has he attacked you. And have you not learned to be on your guard against perversions of Scripture and twistings of God's Word designed to lead you to destruction?

At other times, Satan will use the weapon of our own experience. "Ah!" the devil will say, "on such-and-such a day, you sinned in this way. How can you be a child of God?" At another time he will say, "You are self-righteous; therefore, you cannot be an heir of heaven." Then he will begin to rake up all the old stories that we have long forgotten of all our past unbeliefs, our past wanderings, and so forth, and throw them in our face. He will say, "What! *You*, YOU a Christian? Some Christian you must be!" Or possibly he will begin to tempt you by another's example: "So-and-so is a believer; he did it. Why can't you do the same? So-and-so does it, and he gets by and is just as respected as you are." Be careful, for Satan knows how to choose his weapons! He is not coming out against you, if you are a great giant, with a sling and a stone. He comes armed to the teeth to cut you down. If he knows that you are guarded by a coat of mail that the edge of his sword shall be turned by your armor, he will attack you with deadly poison. And if he knows that you cannot be destroyed by that means, seeing that you have an antidote at hand, he will seek to take you in a trap. And if you are wary, he will send fiery trouble upon you or a crushing avalanche of woe so that he may subdue you. The weapons of his warfare, always evil and often spiritual and unseen, are mighty against such weak creatures as we.

The craftiness of the devil is discovered in another thing—*in the agents the devil employs.* The devil does not do all his dirty work alone; he often employs others to do it for him. When Samson had to be overcome, Satan had a Delilah ready to tempt and lead him astray. Satan knew Samson's heart, where his weakest point was, and he therefore tempted Samson by means of the woman he loved. An old divine says, "There's many a man that has had his head broken by his own rib"; and certainly that is true. Satan has sometimes set a woman's own husband to cast her down to destruction, or he has used some dear friend as the instrument to work his ruin. You remember how David lamented over this evil: "For it was not an enemy that reproached me; then I could have borne it: neither was it he that hated me that did magnify himself against me; . . . But it was thou, a man mine equal, my guide, and mine acquaintance. We took sweet counsel together, and walked unto the house of God in company" (Ps. 55:12–14).

"Ah!" says the devil, "you did not think I was going to send an enemy to speak evil of you, did you? Why, that would not hurt you. I shall choose a friend or an acquaintance; he will come close to you and then stab you in the back." If a minister is to be annoyed, Satan will choose an elder to annoy him. He knows that the minister will not care as much about an attack from any other member of the church, so some elder will lift himself up and domineer over him so that he shall have sleepless nights and anxious days.

The devil is always ready to take in his hand the net into which the fish is most likely to go and to spread the net that is most likely to catch the bird. I do not suspect—if you have believed for a long time—that you will be tempted by a drunk. No, the devil will tempt you by a whining hypocrite. I do not imagine your enemy will attack by way of slander, but your friend may. Satan knows how to use and to disguise all his agents. "Ah!" says he, "a wolf in sheep's clothing will be better for me than a wolf that looks like a wolf; and one in the church will play my game better and accomplish it more readily than one out of it."

Satan proves his craft and cleverness by his choice of agents. It was a cunning thing that he should choose the serpent for the purpose of tempting Eve. Very likely Eve was fascinated by the appearance of the serpent. She probably admired its glossy hue, and we are led to believe that it was a far more noble creature at the time than it is now. Perhaps, then, it could erect itself upon its coils, and Eve was very likely pleased and delighted with it. It would not surprise me if the serpent had been the familiar creature with which Eve played before the devil entered into it.

In a similar way, I know Satan has used me, many times, when he wanted a sharp word to be said against somebody. "Nobody," says the devil, "can hurt or grieve that person better than Mr. Spurgeon. Why, he loves him as his own soul. That's the man to give the unkindest cut of all, and he shall give it." Then I am led, perhaps, to believe some wrong thing against some precious child of God and afterward to speak of it. And then I grieve to think that I should have been so foolish as to lend my heart and tongue to the devil. Let us take heed lest we become instruments of Satan in grieving the hearts of God's people and casting down those who have trouble enough to cast them down without having any from us.

Satan shows his cunning by *the times in which he attacks us.* I thought, when I was sick, that if I could only get up from my bed again and be made strong, I would give the devil a most terrible thrashing for the way he attacked me when I was sick. Coward! Why did he not wait till I was well? But I always find that if my spirits sink and I am in a low condition of heart, Satan specially chooses that time to attack me with unbelief. Let him come upon us when the promise of God is fresh in our memory and we are enjoying a time of sweet outpouring of heart in prayer before God, and he will see how we will fight against him then. But no, he knows that then we have the strength to resist him, and prevailing with God, we should be able to prevail over the devil also. He therefore comes upon us when there is a cloud between ourselves and God. When the body is depressed and the spirits are weak, then will he tempt us and try to lead us to distrust God.

At another time, he will tempt us to pride. Why does he not tempt us to pride when we are sick and depressed in spirit? "No," he says, "I cannot win then." He chooses the time when a man is well, when he is in full enjoyment of the promises and enabled to serve his God with delight, and then he will tempt him to pride. It is the timing of his attacks, the right ordering of his assaults, that makes Satan ten times more terrible an enemy than he would otherwise be, and that proves the depth of his craftiness.

There is one thing about the powers of hell that has always amazed me. The church is always quarrelling, but did you ever hear that the devil and his confederates quarrel? There is a vast host of those fallen spirits, but how marvelously unanimous they are! They are so united that if at any special moment the great black prince of hell wishes to concentrate all the masses of his army at one particular point, it is done to the tick of the clock, and the temptation comes with its fullest force just when he sees it to be the most likely that he will prevail. Ah, if we had such unanimity as that in the church, if we all moved at the guidance of the finger of Christ, if all the church could, at this time, for instance, move in one great mass to attack a certain evil, how much more easily might we prevail! But alas! Satan surpasses us in subtlety, and the powers of hell far exceed us in unanimity. This, however, is a great point in Satan's subtlety, that he always chooses the times of his attacks so wisely.

Satan's subtlety is also very great *in his withdrawings*. When I first joined the church, I could not understand a saying that I heard from an old man that there was no temptation so bad as not being tempted, nor did I understand what Rutherford meant when he said he liked a roaring devil a great deal better than a sleeping devil. I understand it now as described this way: you want to feel, but you do not feel. If you could but doubt, you would think it a very great attainment, and even if you could know the blackness of despair, you would rather feel that than be as you are.

"There!" you say. "I have no doubts about my eternal condition. Somehow, I think I can say, though I could not exactly speak with assurance, for I fear it would be presumption, yet I do trust I can say that I am an heir of heaven. Yet that does not give me any joy. I can go about God's work. I do feel that I love it, yet I cannot feel it is God's work. I seem to have got into a round of duty, till I go on, on, on, like a blind horse that goes because it must go. I read the promise, but I see no particular sweetness in it. In fact, it does not seem as if I need any promise. And even threatenings do not frighten me; there is no terror in them to me. I hear God's Word. I am perhaps stirred by what the minister says, but I do not feel impressed as I should. I feel that I could not live without prayer, and yet there is no unction in my soul. I dare not sin. I trust my life is outwardly blameless. Still, what I have to mourn over is a heavy heart, a lack of spiritual delight or spiritual song, a dead calm in my soul."

There have been times in the past experience of my own soul when I would have been obliged to the devil had he come and stirred me up. I should have felt that God had employed him, against his wish, to do me lasting good, to wake me up to conflict. If the devil would but go into the Enchanted Ground and attack the pilgrims there, what a fine thing it would be for them! But, you will notice, John Bunyan did not put him there, for there was no business for him there. It was in the Valley of Humiliation that there was plenty of work cut out for Satan, but in the Enchanted Ground, the pilgrims were all slumbering, like men asleep on top of the mast. They were drunken with wine so that they could do nothing, and therefore the devil knew he was not needed there; he just left them to sleep on. Madame Bubble and drowsiness would do all his work. But it was in the Valley of Humiliation that he went, and there he had his stern struggle with poor Christian. If you are passing through the land that is enchanted with drowsiness, indifference, and slumber, you will understand the craftiness of the devil in sometimes keeping out of the way.

What Shall We Do with This Enemy?

Our desire is to enter the kingdom of heaven, and we cannot enter it while we stand still. The City of Destruction is behind us, and Death pursues us. We must press toward heaven, but in the way there stands this "roaring lion, seeking whom he may devour." What shall we do? He has great subtlety. How shall we overcome him? Shall we seek to be as subtle as he is? That would be a foolish task; indeed, it would be a sinful one. To seek to be crafty, like the devil, would be as wicked as it would be futile. What shall we do, then? Shall we attack Satan with wisdom? Alas, our wisdom is but folly! "Vain man would be wise," but at his very best, he is but "like a wild ass's colt" (Job 11:12). What, then, shall we do?

The only way to repel Satan's subtlety is *by acquiring true wisdom*. Again I repeat it, man has none of that in himself. What then? Herein is true wisdom. If you would successfully wrestle with Satan, make the Holy Scriptures your daily commune. Out of this sacred Word continually draw your armor and ammunition. Lay hold upon the glorious doctrines of God's Word; make them your daily meat and drink. So shall you be strong to resist the devil, and you shall be joyful in discovering that he will flee from you. "Wherewithal shall a young man cleanse his way," and how shall a Christian guard himself against the enemy? "By taking heed thereto according to thy word" (Ps. 119:9). Let us fight Satan always with an "It is written," for no weapon will ever fight the archenemy as well as Holy Scripture. Attempt to fight Satan with the wooden sword of reason, and he will easily overcome you. But use the blade of God's Word, by which he has been wounded many times, and you will speedily overcome him.

Above all, if we would successfully resist Satan, we must look not merely to revealed wisdom but to *Incarnate Wisdom*. Here must be the chief place of resort for every tempted soul! We must flee to Him "who of God is made unto us wisdom, and righteousness, and sanctification, and redemption" (1 Cor. 1:30). He must teach us, He must guide us, He must be our All-in-all. We must keep close to Him in communion. The sheep are never so safe from the wolf as when they are near the shepherd. We shall never be so secure from the arrows of Satan as when we have our head lying on the Savior's bosom. Believer, walk according to His example, live daily in His fellowship, trust always in His blood, and in this way you shall be more than a conqueror over the subtlety and craft of Satan himself.

It must be a joy to the Christian to know that in the long run, the craft of Satan shall all be defeated and his evil designs against the saints shall prove of no effect. Are you not looking forward to the day when all your temptations are over and you shall land in heaven? And will you not then look down upon this archenemy with holy laughter and derision? While Satan has sought to destroy the living tree, trying to uproot it, he has only been like a gardener digging with his spade and loosening the earth to help the roots to spread themselves. And when he has been with his ax seeking to lop the Lord's trees and mar their beauty, what has he been, after all, but a pruning knife in the hand of God to take away the branches that do not bear fruit and purge those that do bear some that they might bring forth more fruit?

Once upon a time, you know, the church of Christ was like a little brook flowing along in a little narrow dell. Just a few saints were gathered at Jerusalem, and the devil thought, "Now I'll get a great stone and stop the brook from running." So he went and got the great stone and dashed it down into the middle of the brook, thinking, of course, he would stop it from running. Instead of doing so, he scattered the drops all over the world, and each drop became the mother of a fresh fountain. You know what that stone was: it was persecution, and the saints were scattered by it. But then, "Therefore they that were scattered abroad went every where preaching the word" (Acts 8:4), and so the church was multiplied and the devil defeated.

Satan, I tell you to your face, you are the greatest fool that ever breathed, and I will prove it to you in the day when you and I shall stand as enemies—sworn enemies, as we are this day—at the great throne of God; and so, may you say to him when he attacks you. Fear him not, but resist him steadfast in the faith, and you shall prevail.

The great fact of the sufferings of Christ is clearly foretold: "thou shalt bruise his heel." Within the compass of those words we find the whole story of our Lord's sorrows from Bethlehem to Calvary. "It shall bruise thy head": there is the breaking of Satan's regal power, there is the clearing away of sin, there is the destruction of death by resurrection, there is the leading of captivity captive in the ascension, there is the victory of truth in the world through the descent of the Spirit, there is the latter-day glory in which Satan shall be bound, and there is, lastly, the casting of the evil one and his followers into the lake of fire. The conflict and the conquest are both in the compass of these few fruitful words. They may not have been fully understood by those who first heard them, but to us they are full of light. The text at first looks like a flint, hard and cold, but sparks fly from it abundantly, for hidden fires of infinite love and grace lie concealed within.

Chapter Three

Christ the Conqueror of Satan

And I will put enmity between thee and the woman, and between thy seed and her seed; it shall bruise thy head, and thou shalt bruise his heel—Genesis 3:15.

THIS IS THE FIRST GOSPEL sermon ever delivered upon the face of the earth. It was a memorable discourse indeed, with Jehovah Himself for the preacher, and the whole human race and the prince of darkness for the audience. It must be worthy of our heartiest attention.

Is it not remarkable that this great gospel promise should have been delivered so soon after the transgression? As yet no sentence had been pronounced upon either of the two human offenders, but the promise was given under the form of a sentence pronounced upon the serpent. The woman had not yet been condemned to painful travail, or the man to exhausting labor, or even the soil to the curse of thorn and thistle. Before the Lord had said, "Dust thou art, and unto dust thou shalt return" (Gen. 3:19), He was pleased to say that the seed of the woman should bruise the serpent's head. Let us rejoice, then, in the swift mercy of God which, in the early watches of the night of sin, came with comforting words to us.

These words were directed distinctly to the serpent himself and were given as punishment to him for what he had done. It was a day of cruel triumph to him: such joy as his dark mind is capable of had filled him, for he had indulged his malice and gratified his spite. He had in the worst sense destroyed a part of God's works; he had introduced sin into the new world; he had stamped the human race with his own image and gained new forces to promote rebellion and multiply transgression; and therefore he felt that sort of gladness that a fiend can know who bears a hell within him.

But now God comes in, takes up the quarrel personally, and causes the enemy to be disgraced on the very battlefield where he had gained a temporary success. He tells the dragon that this quarrel shall be not between the serpent and man but between God and the serpent. God says solemnly, "I will put enmity between thee and the woman, between thy seed and her seed," and promises that there shall rise in the fullness of time a Champion who, though He suffer, shall smite in a vital part the power of evil, bruising the serpent's head. This was a message of mercy to Adam and Eve because they knew that the tempter would be punished, and as that punishment would involve blessing for them, the vengeance due to the serpent was the guarantee of mercy to themselves. Perhaps, however, by thus obliquely giving the promise, the Lord meant to say, "Not for your sakes do I this, O fallen man and woman, nor for the sake of your descendants, but for My own name and honor's sake, that it be not profaned among the fallen spirits. I will repair the damage caused by the tempter, that My name and My glory may not be diminished among the immortal spirits who look down upon the scene." All this would be very humbling but yet consolatory to our parents if they thought of it, seeing that the divine sovereignty and glory afford us a stronger foundation of hope than human merit, even if merit can be supposed to exist.

Now we must note that this first gospel sermon was the earliest believers' primary hope. This was all that Adam had by way of revelation and all that Abel had received. This one lone star shone in Abel's sky; Abel looked up to it and he believed. By its light he spelled out "sacrifice" and therefore brought of the firstlings of his flock and laid them upon the altar, proving in his own person how the seed of the serpent hated the seed of the woman, for his brother slew him for his testimony. Although Enoch, the seventh from

Adam, prophesied concerning the second advent, he does not appear to have uttered anything new concerning the first coming, so that still this one promise remained as man's sole word of hope. The torch that flamed within the gates of Eden just before man was driven forth lit up the world to all believers until the Lord was pleased to give more light, renewing and enlarging the revelation of His covenant when He spoke with His servant Noah. Those ancient fathers who lived before the flood rejoiced in the mysterious language of our text, and resting on it, they died in faith.

It was by no means a slender revelation, for it is wonderfully full of meaning. There lies within it—as an oak lies within an acorn—all the great truth that makes up the gospel of Christ. Observe that here is the grand mystery of the incarnation. Christ is that seed of the woman who is spoken of, and there is a hint not darkly given as to how that incarnation should be effected. Jesus was not born after the ordinary manner of the sons of men. Mary was overshadowed by the Holy Ghost, and "the holy thing" that was born of her was as to His humanity the seed of the woman only, as it is written, "Behold, a virgin shall conceive and bear a son, and shall call his name Immanuel" (Isa. 7:14). The promise plainly teaches that the Deliverer would be born of a woman, and carefully viewed, it also foreshadows the divine method of the Redeemer's conception and birth. So also is the doctrine of the two seeds plainly taught: "I will put enmity between thee and the woman, and between thy seed and her seed." There was evidently to be in the world a seed of the woman on God's side against the serpent and a seed of the serpent that should always be on the evil side even as it is this day. The church of God and the synagogue of Satan both exist. We see an Abel and a Cain, an Isaac and an Ishmael, a Jacob and an Esau. Those who are born after the flesh—being the children of their father the devil—do Satan's works, but those who are born again—being born after the Spirit, after the power of the life of Christ—are in Christ Jesus, the seed of the woman, and contend earnestly against the dragon and his seed.

Here, too, the great fact of the sufferings of Christ is clearly foretold: "thou shalt bruise his heel." Within the compass of those words we find the whole story of our Lord's sorrows from Bethlehem to Calvary. "It shall bruise thy head": there is the breaking of Satan's regal power, there is the clearing away of sin, there is the destruction of death by resurrection, there is the leading of captivity captive in the ascension, there is the victory of truth in the world through the descent of the Spirit, there is the latter-day glory in which Satan shall be bound, and there is, lastly, the casting of the evil one and his followers into the lake of fire. The conflict and the conquest are both in the compass of these few fruitful words. They may not have been fully understood by those who first heard them, but to us they are full of light. The text at first looks like a flint, hard and cold, but sparks fly from it abundantly, for hidden fires of infinite love and grace lie concealed within.

We do not know what our first parents understood by it, but we may be certain that they gathered a great amount of comfort from it. They must have understood that they were not then and there to be destroyed, because the Lord had spoken of a "seed." They would argue that it was needful that Eve should live if there should be a seed from her. They understood, too, that if that seed was to overcome the serpent and bruise his head, it must mean good to themselves. They could not fail to see that there was some great, mysterious benefit to be conferred upon them by the victory that their seed would achieve over the instigator of their ruin. They went on in faith upon this and were comforted in travail and in toil, and I do not doubt that both Adam and Eve entered into everlasting rest through this promise.

I shall handle this text in three ways. First, we shall notice *its facts*; second, we shall consider *the experience within the heart of each believer that tallies to those facts*; and third, we shall discuss *the encouragement* that the text and its connection as a whole bring to us.

The Facts

The first fact is that *enmity was promised*. The text begins, "I will put enmity between thee and the woman." The woman and the serpent had been very friendly; they had conversed together. The woman thought at the time that the serpent was her friend, and she was so much his friend that she took his advice in the face of God's precept and was willing to believe bad things about the great Creator because of the insinuations of this wicked, crafty serpent. The moment that God spoke, the friendship between the woman and the serpent had already in a measure ended, for the woman had accused the serpent to God and said, "The serpent beguiled me, and I did eat." So far, so good. The friendship of sinners does not last long. The friends have already begun to quarrel, and now the Lord comes in and graciously takes advantage of the quarrel and says, "I will carry this disagreement a good deal further, I will put enmity between you." Satan counted on man's descendants being his confederates, but God would break up this covenant and raise up a seed that should war against the satanic power. Thus, we have God's first declaration that He will set up a rival kingdom to oppose the tyranny of sin and Satan, that He will create in the hearts of a chosen seed an enmity against evil so that they shall fight against it and with many struggles and pain shall overcome the prince of darkness. The divine Spirit has abundantly achieved this plan and purpose of the Lord, combatting the fallen angel by a glorious man, making man to be Satan's foe and conqueror.

Henceforth the woman was to hate the evil one. She had abundant cause for so doing, and as often as she thought of him, it would be with infinite regret that she could have listened to his malicious and deceitful talk. The woman's seed has also evermore had enmity against the evil one. I do not mean the carnal seed, for Paul tells us, "They which are the children of the flesh, these are not the children of God: but the children of the promise are counted for the seed" (Rom. 9:8). The carnal seed of the man and woman are not meant, but the spiritual seed, even Christ Jesus and those who are in Him. Wherever you meet these, they hate the serpent with a perfect hatred. We would if we could destroy from our souls every work of Satan, and out of this poor afflicted world of ours we would root up every evil that Satan has planted. That seed of the woman, that glorious *One*, you know how He abhorred the devil and all his schemes. There was enmity between Christ and Satan, for Christ came to destroy the works of the devil and to deliver those who are under bondage to him. For that purpose He was born, He lived, He died, He has gone into the glory, and for that purpose He will come again to find out His adversary and utterly destroy him and his works everywhere from among the sons of men. This putting of the enmity between the two seeds was the commencement of the plan of mercy, the first act in the program of grace. Of the woman's seed it was henceforth said, "Thou lovest righteousness, and hatest wickedness: therefore God, thy God, hath anointed thee with the oil of gladness above thy fellows" (Ps. 45:7).

Then comes the second prophecy, which has also turned into a fact, namely, *the coming of the Champion.* The seed of the woman by promise is to champion the cause and oppose the dragon. That seed is the Lord Jesus. The prophet Micah said, "But thou, Bethlehem Ephratah, though thou be little among the thousands of Judah, yet out of thee shall he come forth unto me that is to be ruler in Israel; whose goings forth have been from of old, from everlasting. Therefore will he give them up, until the time that she which travaileth hath brought forth" (Mic. 5:2–3). To none other than the babe who was born in Bethlehem of the blessed Virgin can the words of prophecy refer. And it is concerning her son that we sing, "For unto us a child is born, unto us a son is given: . . . and his name shall be called Wonderful, Counsellor, The mighty God, The everlasting Father, The Prince of Peace" (Isa. 9:6).

On the memorable night at Bethlehem, when angels sang in heaven, the seed of the woman appeared, and as soon as He saw the light, the old serpent, the devil, entered into the heart of Herod if possible to slay Him, but the Father preserved Him. As soon as He publicly came forward upon the stage of action, thirty years later, Satan met Him with the temptation in the wilderness, and there the woman's seed fought with him who was a liar from the beginning. The devil assailed Him three times with all the artillery of flattery, malice, craft, and falsehood, but the peerless Champion stood unwounded and chased his foeman from the field. Then our Lord set up His kingdom and carried the war into the enemy's country. He spoke to the wicked and unclean spirit and said, "I charge thee come out of him," and the demon was expelled. Legions of devils flew before Him: they sought to hide themselves in swine to escape the terror of His presence. "Art thou come hither to torment us before the time?" (Matt. 8:29) was their cry when the wonder-working Christ dislodged them from the bodies that they tormented. And He made His disciples mighty against the evil one, for in His name they cast out devils, till Jesus said, "I beheld Satan as lightning fall from heaven" (Luke 10:18).

Then there came a second personal conflict—Gethsemane's sorrows, which I take it were to a great degree caused by a personal assault of Satan, for our Master said, "This is your hour, and the power of darkness" (Luke 22:53). He said also, "The prince of this world cometh" (John 14:30). What a struggle it was. Though Satan had nothing in Christ, yet did he seek if possible to lead Him away from completing His great sacrifice, and there did our Master sweat as it were great drops of blood in the agony that cost Him to contend with the fiend. Then it was that our Champion began the last fight of all on the cross and won it to the bruising of the serpent's head. Nor did He end till He had spoiled principalities and powers and openly made a show of them.

The conflict of our glorious Lord continues in His seed. We preach Christ crucified, and every sermon shakes the gates of hell. We bring sinners to Jesus by the Spirit's power, and every convert is a stone torn down from the wall of Satan's mighty castle. And the day shall come when the evil one shall be overcome everywhere, and the words of John in the Revelation shall be fulfilled:

> And the great dragon was cast out, that old serpent, called the Devil, and Satan, which deceiveth the whole world: he was cast out into the earth, and his angels were cast out with him. And I heard a loud voice saying in heaven, Now is come salvation, and strength, and the kingdom of our God, and the power of his Christ: for the accuser of our brethren is cast down, which accused them before our God day and night" (Rev. 12:9–10).

The Champion has come, the man-child has been born, and though the dragon is wroth with the woman and makes war with the remnant of her seed that keeps the testimony of Jesus Christ, yet the battle is the Lord's, and the victory falls to Him whose name is Faithful and True.

The third fact that comes out in the text is that *our Champion's heel should be bruised*. You know how all His life long He was perpetually being made to suffer. He carried our sicknesses and our sorrows. But the bruising came mainly when both in body and in mind His whole human nature was made to agonize, when His soul was exceedingly sorrowful even unto death, and His enemies pierced His hands and feet, and He endured the shame and pain of death by crucifixion. Look at your Master and King upon the cross, all distained with blood and dust! There was His heel most cruelly bruised. When they take down that precious body and wrap it in fair white linen and spices and lay it in Joseph's tomb, they weep as they handle that body in which the Deity had dwelt, for there again Satan had bruised His heel. It was not merely that God had bruised Him—"yet it pleased the LORD to bruise him" (Isa. 53:10)—but the devil let loose Herod, Pilate, Caiaphas, the Jews, and the Romans—all of them his tools—upon Him whom he knew to be the Christ, so that He was bruised by the old serpent.

That is all, however! It is only His heel, not His head, that is bruised! For lo, the Champion rises again; the bruise was neither mortal nor continual. Though He dies, yet still so brief is the interval in which He slumbers in the tomb that His holy body has not seen corruption, and He comes forth perfect and lovely in His manhood, rising from His grave as from a refreshing sleep after so long a day of unresting toil! Jesus only retains a scar in His heel, and that He bears to the skies as His glory and beauty. Before the throne He looks like a lamb that has been slain, but in the power of an endless life He lives to God.

Then comes the fourth fact, namely, that while His heel was being bruised, *He was to bruise the serpent's head*. By His sufferings, Christ has overthrown Satan; by the heel that was bruised, He has trodden upon the head that devised the bruising. Though Satan is not dead, yet Christ has so far broken Satan's head that Satan has missed his mark altogether. Satan intended to make the human race the captives of his power, but it is redeemed from his iron yoke. God has delivered many of them, and the day shall come when He will cleanse the whole earth from the serpent's slimy trail so that the entire world shall be full of the praises of God. Satan thought that this world would be the arena of his victory over God and good, instead of which it is already the grandest theater of divine wisdom, love, grace, and power. Even heaven itself is not so resplendent with mercy as is the earth, for it is here the Savior poured out His blood.

Moreover, Satan thought, no doubt, that when he had led our race astray and brought death upon it, he had effectually marred the Lord's work. He rejoiced that it would pass under the cold seal of death and that all the earthly bodies would rot in the grave. Had he not spoiled the handiwork of his great Lord? God may make man as a marvelous creature, and He may put into His nostrils the breath of life, but, "Ah," says Satan, "I have infused a poison into him that will make him return to the dust."

But now, behold, our Champion has risen from the dead and given a pledge that all His followers shall rise from the dead also. Thus is Satan foiled, for death shall not retain a bone, nor a piece of a bone, of one of those who belonged to the woman's seed. At the trump of the archangel from the earth and sea they shall arise, and this shall be their shout: "O death, where is thy sting? O grave, where is thy victory?" (1 Cor. 15:55). Satan, knowing this, feels already that by the resurrection his head is broken. Glory be to the Christ of God for this!

In multitudes of other ways the devil has been vanquished by our Lord Jesus, and so shall he ever be till he shall be cast into the lake of fire.

How This Relates to Our Experience

The first thing Christ does is come to us in mercy and *put enmity between us and the serpent*. That is the very first work of grace. There once was peace between us and Satan; when Satan tempted we yielded; whatever he taught us we believed; we were his willing slaves. But perhaps you can recall when you first began to feel dissatisfied; the world's pleasures no longer pleased you; all the juice seemed to have been taken out of the apple, and you had nothing left but the hard core. Then you suddenly perceived that you were living in sin, and you were miserable about it, and though you could not get rid of sin, yet you hated it and sighed over it and cried and groaned. In your heart of hearts you remained no longer on the devil's side, for you began to cry, "O wretched man that I am! who shall deliver me from the body of this death?" (Rom. 7:24). The Lord in infinite mercy had begun to drop the divine life into your soul. You did not know it, but there it was, a spark of the celestial fire, the living and incorruptible seed that abides forever. The more you could not bear sin, the more you hated the thought of it. So it was with you. Is it so now? Is there still enmity between you and the serpent? Indeed you are more and more the sworn enemy of evil, and you willingly acknowledge it.

Then came the Champion: that is to say, "Christ in you, the hope of glory" (Col. 1:27). You heard of Him, and you understood the truth about Him, and it seemed a wonderful thing that He should be your substitute to bear your sin and all its curse and punishment, and that He should give to you His righteousness—yes, and His very self—that you might be saved. You saw how sin could be overthrown, did you not? As soon as your heart understood Christ, you saw that what the law could not do—in that it was weak through the flesh—Christ was able to accomplish, and that the power of sin and Satan under which you had been in bondage, and which you now loathed, could and would be broken and destroyed because Christ had come into the world to overcome it.

Do you recall how you were led to see *the bruising of Christ's heel* and to stand in wonder and observe what the enmity of the serpent had wrought in Him? Did you not begin to feel the bruised heel yourself? Did not sin torment you? Did not the very thought of it trouble you? Did not your own heart become a plague to you? Did not Satan begin to tempt you? Did he not inject blasphemous thoughts and urge you on to desperate measures? Did he not question the mercy of God and the possibility of your salvation, and so on? This was his nibbling at *your* heel. He is at his old tricks still. He worries those whom he cannot devour with a malicious joy. Did not your worldly friends begin to annoy you? Did they not give you the cold shoulder because they saw something about you so strange and foreign to their tastes? Did they not call your conduct fanaticism, pride, obstinacy, bigotry? This persecution is the serpent's seed beginning to discover the woman's seed and to carry on the old war. What does Paul say? "But as then he that was born after the flesh persecuted him that was born after the Spirit, even so it is now" (Gal. 4:29). True godliness is an unnatural and strange thing to them, and the enmity of the human heart toward Christ and His seed is always the same and very often shows itself in "trials of cruel mockings," which to tender hearts are very hard to bear. This is your heel being bruised in sympathy with the bruising of the heel of the glorious seed of the woman.

But do you know something of the other fact, namely, that *we conquer, for the serpent's head is broken in us*? Is not the power and dominion of sin broken in you? Do you not feel that you cannot sin because you are born of God? Some sins that were masters to you once do not trouble you now. The cure of divine grace is very wonderful and complete. We have known persons delivered from unclean living, and they have at once become chaste and pure because Christ has smitten the old dragon with such blows that he could not have power over them in that respect. The chosen seed sin and mourn it, but they are not slaves of sin; their heart does not go after it. They, like Paul, have to say sometimes, "the evil which I would not, that I do" (Rom. 7:19), but they are wretched when it is so. They consent with their heart to the law of God that is good, and they sigh and cry that they may be helped to obey it, for they are no longer under the slavery of sin. The serpent's reigning power and dominion are broken in them.

Satan's power is broken next in this way—that guilt of sin is gone. The great power of the serpent lies in unpardoned sin. Satan cries, "I have made you guilty: I brought you under the curse." "No," say we, "we are delivered from the curse and are now blessed, for it is written, 'Blessed is he whose transgression is forgiven, whose sin is covered' (Ps. 32:1). We are no longer guilty, for who shall lay anything to the charge of God's elect? Since Christ hath justified, who is he that condemneth?" Here is a swinging blow for the old dragon's head, such as he will not recover from.

The Lord also grants us to know what it is to overcome temptation and so to break the head of the fiend. Satan allures us with many baits. He has studied our points well, he knows the weakness of the flesh; but many times, blessed be God, we have foiled him completely to his eternal shame! How must the devil have felt that day when he tried to overthrow Job, dragged him down to the dunghill, robbed him of everything, covered him with sores, and yet could not make him yield! Job conquered when he cried, "Though he slay me, yet will I trust in him" (Job 13:15). A feeble man had vanquished a devil who could raise the wind and blow down a house, destroying the family who were feasting in it. Devil as he is and crowned prince of the power of the air, yet the poor bereaved patriarch sitting on the dunghill covered with sores, being one of the woman's seed, through the strength of the inner life won the victory over him.

Moreover, we have this ultimate hope that the very taint of sin in us will be destroyed. The day will come when we shall be without spot or wrinkle or any such thing, and we shall stand before the throne of God, having suffered no injury whatever from the fall and from all the schemes of Satan, "for they are without fault before the throne of God" (Rev. 14:5). What triumph that will be! "And the God of peace shall bruise Satan under your feet shortly" (Rom. 16:20). When He has made you perfect, as He will do, you have bruised the serpent's head indeed.

Your resurrection, too, when Satan shall see you come up from the grave like one that has been perfumed in a bath of spices, when he shall see you arise in the image of Christ, with the same body that was sown in corruption and weakness raised in incorruption and power, then will he feel an infinite chagrin and know that his head is bruised by the woman's seed.

I should add that every time we are made useful in saving souls we repeat the bruising of the serpent's head. When you go, dear sister, among the poor children and pick them up from where they are Satan's prey, and when through your means, by the grace of God, the little wanderers become children of God, then you in your measure bruise the old serpent's head. When by preaching the gospel we turn sinners from the error of their ways so that they escape from the power of darkness, again we bruise the serpent's head. Whenever in any shape or way you are blessed to the aiding of the cause of truth and righteousness in the world, you, too, tread upon his head. In all deliverances and victories, you overcome and prove the promise true: "Thou shalt tread upon the lion and adder: the young lion and the dragon shalt thou trample under feet. Because he hath set his love upon me, therefore will I deliver him: I will set him on high, because he hath known my name" (Ps. 91:13–14).

The Encouragement

I want you to exercise faith in the promise and be comforted. The text evidently encouraged Adam very much. I do not think we have attached enough importance to the conduct of Adam after the Lord had spoken to him. Notice the simple but conclusive proof that he gave of his faith. Sometimes an action may seem small and unimportant and yet it may display the whole state of the man's mind. Adam acted in faith upon what God said, for we read, "And Adam called his wife's name Eve [or Life]; because she was the mother of all living" (Gen. 3:20). Eve was not a mother at all, but as the life was to come through her by virtue of the promised seed, Adam makes his full conviction of the truth of the promise, though at the time the woman had borne no children. There stood trembling Adam, fresh from the awful presence of God, and Adam turns to his fellow culprit as she stands there trembling, too, and he calls her Eve, mother of the life that is yet to be. It was grandly spoken by Father Adam. Had Adam been left to himself, he would have murmured, or at least despaired; but no, his faith in the new promise gave him hope. Neither Adam nor Eve utter a word of protest against God's condemnation; they both accept the well-deserved sentence with the silence that denotes the perfection of their resignation; their only word is full of simple faith. There was no child on whom to set their hopes, nor would the true seed be born for many ages. Still, Eve is to be the mother of all living, and Adam calls her so.

Following their example, let us exercise this same faith in the wider revelation that God has given and always extract the utmost comfort from it. Make a point, whenever you receive a promise from God, to get all you can out of it. If you carry out that rule, it is wonderful what comfort you will gain. Some go on the principle of getting as little as possible out of God's Word. I believe that such a plan is the proper way with a man's word. Always understand it at the minimum, because that is what he means, but God's Word is to be understood at the maximum, for He will do exceedingly abundantly above what you ask or even think.

Notice by way of further encouragement that we may regard our reception of Christ's righteousness as an installment of the final overthrow of the devil. Genesis 3:21 says, "Unto Adam also and to his wife did the LORD God make coats of skins, and clothed them." A very condescending, thoughtful, and instructive deed of divine love! God heard what Adam said to his wife and saw that he was a believer, and so He gives him the type of perfect righteousness that is the believer's portion—He covered him with lasting raiment. No more fig leaves, which were a mere mockery, but a close-fitting garment that had been procured through the death of a victim. The Lord brings that and puts it on him, and Adam could no more say, "I am naked." How could he, for God had clothed him. Now, let us take out of the promise that is given us concerning our Lord's conquest over the devil this one item and rejoice in it, for Christ has delivered us from the power of the serpent who opened our eyes and told us we were naked, by covering us from head to foot with a righteousness that adorns and protects us so that we are comfortable in heart and beautiful in the sight of God and are no more ashamed.

By way of encouragement in pursuing the Christian life, I would say to expect to be assailed. If you have fallen into trouble through being a Christian, be encouraged by it. Do not at all regret or fear it, but rejoice in that day and leap for joy, for this is the constant token of the covenant. If you do not experience any of the enmity, you might begin to fear that you are on the wrong side. When you come under the sneer of sarcasm and oppression, rejoice and triumph, for you are partakers with the glorious seed of the woman in the bruising of His heel.

Still further encouragement comes from this. Your suffering as a Christian is not brought upon you for your own sake. You are partners with the great seed of the woman; you are confederates with Christ. You should not think the devil cares much about you: the battle is against Christ in you. If you were not in Christ, the devil would never trouble you. When you were without Christ in the world, you might have sinned as you like, but now the serpent's seed hates Christ in you. This exalts the sufferings of persecution to a position far above all common afflictions. If Christ is in you, nothing will dismay you, but by faith you will overcome the world, the flesh, and the devil.

Last of all, let us resist the devil's knowing that he has received a broken head. I am inclined to think that Martin Luther's way of laughing at the devil was a very good one, for the devil is worthy of shame and everlasting contempt. Luther once threw an inkstand at Satan's head when Satan was tempting him very sorely, and though the act itself appears absurd enough, yet it was a true type of what that greater Reformer was all his life long, for the books he wrote were truly a flinging of the inkstand at the head of the fiend. That is what we have to do: we are to resist him by every means. Let us do this bravely and tell him to his face that we are not afraid of him. Tell him to remember his bruised head, which he tries to cover with a crown of pride. We know him and see the deadly wound he bears. His power is gone; he is fighting a lost battle; he is contending against omnipotence. He has set himself against the oath of the Father, against the blood of the incarnate Son, against the eternal power and Godhead of the blessed Spirit, all of which are engaged in the defense of the seed of the woman in the day of battle. Therefore, be steadfast in resisting the evil one, be strong in faith, and give glory to God.

Instrumental in the fall of humanity, Satan has acquired a very vast experience in opposing mankind. Having tempted the highest and the lowest, he knows exceedingly well what the strings of human action are and how to play upon them. He watches first of all our peculiar weaknesses. He looks us up and down and soon discovers our faults. Our weakness may be pride or lust or impatience or laziness, but we are assured that the eye of malice is quick to perceive and take advantage of a weakness. When the arch-spy finds a weak place in the wall of our castle, he takes care to plant his battering ram and begin his seige. You may conceal—even from your dearest friend—your weakness, but you will not conceal it from your worst enemy, who has lynx eyes and detects in a moment the joint in your armor.

Chapter Four

Satan Considering the Saints

And the LORD said unto Satan, Hast thou considered my servant Job?—Job 1:8.

HOW VERY UNCERTAIN are all the things of this world! How foolish it is to lay up treasure anywhere except in heaven! Job's prosperity promised as much stability as anything beneath the moon. The man had a large household of devoted servants and an accumulated wealth that does not suddenly depreciate in value—oxen, asses, and cattle. He carried on the business of agriculture on a very large scale and probably raised everything that his establishment required. His children were numerous enough to promise a long line of descendants. His prosperity lacked nothing for its consolidation. It had come to its high-water mark. Where was the cause that could make it ebb?

Up there, beyond the clouds, where no human eye could see, there was a scene enacted that would have a profound impact on Job's prosperity. The spirit of evil stood face to face with the infinite Spirit of all good, and we overhear the extraordinary conversation that took place. When called to account for his doings, the evil one boasted that he had gone to and fro throughout the earth, insinuating that he had met with no hindrance to his will and had found no one to oppose his freely moving and acting at his own pleasure.

He had marched everywhere like a king in his own dominion, unhindered and unchallenged. When the great God reminded him that there was at least one place among men where he had no foothold and his power was unrecognized—namely, in the heart of Job—that there was one man who stood like an impregnable castle, garrisoned by integrity and held with perfect loyalty as the possession of the King of Heaven, the evil one defied Jehovah to test the faithfulness of Job, told Him that the patriarch's integrity was due to his prosperity, that he served God and shunned evil from impure motives because he found his conduct profitable to himself. The God of heaven took up the challenge and gave the evil one permission to take away all the mercies affirmed to be the props of Job's integrity, to pull down all the supports and see whether the tower would not stand in its own inherent strength. In consequence of this, all Job's wealth went in one black day, and not even a child was left to whisper comfort. A second interview between the Lord and his fallen angel took place. Job was again the subject of conversation, and the Great One, defied by Satan, permitted Satan even to touch Job in his bone and flesh till the prince became worse than a pauper and he who was rich and happy was poor and wretched, filled with disease from head to foot, and left to scrape himself with a miserable potsherd to gain a slight relief from his pain.

We see in this the temporariness of all earthly things. "For he hath founded it upon the seas" (Ps. 24:2) is David's description of this world; and, if the world is founded on the seas, can you wonder that it changes so often? Never put your trust in anything beneath the stars. Remember that "Change" is stamped on this world. Do not say, "My mountain standeth firm: it shall never be moved." The glance of Jehovah's eye can shake your mountain into dust; the touch of His foot can make it like Sinai, to melt like wax and billow with smoke. "Set your affection on things above . . . where Christ sitteth on the right hand of God" (Col. 3:2, 1), and let your heart and treasure be "where neither moth nor rust doth corrupt, and where thieves do not break through nor steal" (Matt. 6:20). The words of Bernard may here instruct us: "That is the true and chief joy which is not conceived from the creature, but received from the Creator, which none can take from thee: compared with which all other pleasure is torment, all joy is grief, sweet things are bitter, all glory is baseness, and all delectable things are despicable."

Accept this much as merely an introduction to our primary discourse. The Lord said to Satan, "Hast thou considered my servant Job?" Let us deliberate, first, *in what sense the evil spirit may be said to consider the people of God*; second, *what it is that he considers about them*; and third, *let us comfort ourselves by the reflection that one who is far above Satan considers us in a higher sense.*

How Satan Considers the People of God

The usual biblical meaning of the word *consider* is seen in such verses as "O Lord consider my trouble" (Ps. 9:13) and "Consider my meditation" (Ps. 5:1). Such consideration implies goodwill and a careful inspection of the object of benevolence with regard to a wise distribution of favor. In that sense, Satan never considers anyone. If he has any benevolence, it is toward himself, but all his consideration of others is of the most spiteful kind. No meteoric flash of good flits across the black midnight of his soul. Nor does he consider us as we are told to consider the works of God, that is, to derive instruction as to God's wisdom and love and kindness. He does not honor God by what he sees in His works or in His people. Instead he considers the Christian and becomes more foolishly God's enemy than he was before. *He regards believers with wonder when he considers the difference between them and himself.* A traitor, when he knows the thorough villainy and blackness of his own heart, cannot help being astounded when he is forced to believe another man is faithful. The first resort of a treacherous heart is to believe that all men would be just as treacherous and are really so at bottom. The traitor thinks that all men are traitors like himself—or would be if it paid them better than fidelity.

When Satan looks at the believer and finds him faithful to God and His truth, he perhaps despises him for his folly yet marvels at him and wonders how he can act like this. "I," he seems to say, "a prince, a peer of God's parliament, would not submit *my* will to Jehovah: I thought it better to reign in hell than serve in heaven: how is it that these faithful ones stand? What grace is it that keeps them faithful? I, a vessel of gold, was broken; these believers are earthen vessels, but I cannot break them! I could not stand in my glory—what can be the matchless grace that upholds them in their poverty, obscurity, persecution, still faithful to the God who does not bless and exalt them as He did me!"

It may be that Satan also wonders at the believer's happiness. He feels within himself a seething sea of misery. There is an unfathomable gulf of anguish within his soul, and when he looks at believers, he sees them full of peace and happiness and often without any outward means by which they should be comforted, yet rejoicing and full of glory. *He* goes up and down through the world and possesses great power, and there are many soldiers to serve him, yet he lacks the happiness of spirit possessed by the humble peasant, obscure, unknown, having no servants to wait upon her, but stretched upon a bed of sickness. He admires and hates the peace that reigns in the believer's soul.

Satan's consideration may go further than this. Do you not think that *Satan considers believers to detect, if possible, any flaw in them by way of comfort to himself?* "*They* are not pure," says he. "*They* still sin! These adopted children of God, for whom the glorious Son bowed his head and gave up the ghost—even they offend!" How he must chuckle, with such delight as he is capable of, over the secret sins of God's people, and if he can see anything in them inconsistent with their profession, anything that appears to be deceitful—and therein like himself—he rejoices. Each sin born in the believer's heart cries to him, "My father! my father!" and he feels something like the joy of fatherhood as he sees his foul offspring. He looks at the carnality in the Christian and admires the tenacity with which it maintains its hold, the force and vehemence with which it struggles for the mastery, the craft and cunning with which every now and then, at convenient opportunities, it puts forth all its force. He considers the believer's inconsistency and impurity and makes it one of the books in which he diligently reads. In this respect he had very little to consider in God's true servant, Job.

Nor is this all, but rather just the starting point of his consideration. Surely *he views the Lord's people, and especially the more eminent and excellent among them, as the great barriers to the progress of his kingdom.* Satan must have thought much of Martin Luther. "I could ride the world over," says he, "if it were not for him. He stands in my way. If I could get rid of him, I would not mind though fifty thousand smaller saints stood in my way." He is sure to consider God's servant if there is "none like him," if he stands out distinct and separate from his fellows. Those called to the work of the ministry must expect from their position to be Satan's special targets. When the glass is at the eye of that dreadful warrior, he is sure to look for the officers, and he bids his sharpshooters to be very careful to aim at them, for, says he, "If the standard-bearer falls, then shall the victory be more quickly gained and our opponents put to rout."

The nearer you live to God, the more you can expect Satan's opposition. There is sure to be a contention wherever the harvest is plenteous and where the farmer's toil is well rewarded. Satan, if he can, wants to pluck God's jewels from His crown and take the Redeemer's precious stones even from the breastplate itself. He views them as hindrances to his reign and contrives methods by which he may move them out of his way or even turn them to his own purposes. Darkness would cover the earth if he could blow out the lights; hence his perpetual consideration is to make the faithful fail from among men.

It does not require much wisdom to discern that *the great object of Satan in considering God's people is to do them harm.* I do not think Satan hopes to destroy God's elect. Satan has been foiled so often when he has attacked God's people that he can hardly think he shall be able to destroy the elect. Because his black eye can never peer into God's book of secret decrees, it seems to me that he makes it his policy to attack all the people of God with vehemence—not knowing where he may succeed. He goes about seeking whom he *may* devour. And he does not do it alone. I do not know that many of us have ever been tempted directly by Satan. We may not be notable enough among men to be worth *his* trouble, but he has a whole host of inferior spirits under his supremacy and control. Thus, all the servants of God come under the direct or indirect assaults of the great enemy of souls, and that with a view to destroying them, for he would, if it were possible, deceive the very elect.

Where he cannot destroy, there is no doubt that Satan's object is to cause worry. Satan hates to see God's people happy. I believe the devil greatly delights in pastors whose preaching multiplies and fosters doubts and fears, grief and despondency, as the evidences of God's people. "Ah," the devil says, "preach on; you are doing my work well. If I can make them hang their harps on the willows and go about with miserable faces, I reckon I have done my work very completely." Beware of those temptations that pretend to make us humble but really aim at making us unbelieving. Our God takes no delight in mistrust. Banish all your ill surmisings and rejoice in unmoved confidence.

God delights to be worshipped with joy. "O come, let us sing unto the LORD: let us make a joyful noise to the rock of our salvation. Let us come before his presence with thanksgiving" (Ps. 95:1–2). Satan despises this. Martin Luther used to say, "Let us sing psalms and spite the devil." I have no doubt he was right, for that lover of discord hates harmonious, joyous praise. The archenemy wants to make you wretched here if he cannot have you hereafter, and in this he is aiming a blow at the honor of God. He is well aware that mournful Christians often dishonor the faithfulness of God by mistrusting, and if he can worry us until we no more believe in the constancy and goodness of the Lord, he has robbed God of His praise. "He that offereth praise, glorifieth me," says God (Ps. 50:23), and so Satan lays the ax at the root of our praise.

Moreover, if Satan cannot destroy a believer, how often has he *spoiled the believer's usefulness*? Many have fallen—not to break their neck but to break an important bone—and have gone limping to their grave! We recall with grief some who ran well but through stress of temptation fell into sin, and their names were never mentioned in the church again, except with bated breath. All thought and hoped they were saved as by fire, but certainly their former usefulness never could return. It is very easy to go back in the heavenly pilgrimage, but it is very hard to retrieve your steps. Watch for attacks and stand fast, because you, as a pillar in the house of God, are very dear to other believers. As fathers or mothers, we do not wish to be grieved by hearing the victory shouts of our adversaries over you. May God grant us grace to stand against the wiles of Satan, that having done his worst he may gain no advantage over us, and after having considered and counted well our towers and bulwarks, he may be compelled to retreat because his battering rams cannot jar so much as a stone from their ramparts.

Why is it that God permits this constant and malevolent consideration of his people? One answer, doubtless, is that God knows what is for His own glory, that having permitted free agency and the existence of evil, it does not seem agreeable with His having done so to destroy Satan. But God gives Satan power that it may be a fair hand-to-hand fight between sin and holiness, between grace and deceitfulness. Besides, let it be remembered that the temptations of Satan can work to the service of God's people. Fenelon, the French prelate and writer, says Satan's temptations are the file that rubs off much of the rust of self-confidence. Temptations are the horrible sound in the soldier's ear that is sure to keep the soldier awake. Without temptation, flesh and blood are weak—and though the spirit may be willing, yet we may be found falling asleep. Children do not run away from their father's side when big dogs bark at them. The howlings of the devil may tend to drive us nearer to Christ, teaching us our own weakness and keeping up our vigilance. "Be sober, be vigilant; because your adversary the devil, as a roaring lion, walketh about, seeking whom he may devour" (1 Pet. 5:8). Those in ministry positions should affectionately press one earnest request upon their congregations: "Brethren, pray for us," that, exposed peculiarly to the consideration of Satan, they may be guarded by divine power.

What Satan Purposes Toward God's People

Instrumental in the fall of humanity, Satan has acquired a very vast experience in opposing mankind. Having tempted the highest and the lowest, he knows exceedingly well what the strings of human action are and how to play upon them. He watches first of all *our peculiar weaknesses*. He looks us up and down and soon discovers our faults. Our weakness may be pride or lust or impatience or laziness, but we are assured that the eye of malice is quick to perceive and take advantage of a weakness. When the arch-spy finds a weak place in the wall of our castle, he takes care to plant his battering ram and begin his seige. You may conceal—even from your dearest friend—your weakness, but you will not conceal it from your worst enemy, who has lynx eyes and detects in a moment the joint in your armor.

Satan also considers *our attitudes and states of mind*. He knows when our mind is in a mood where we would be more than a match for him, and he shuns the encounter. Some people are more open to temptation's attack when they are distressed and depressed. Others will be more liable to take fire when they are jubilant and full of joy. Certain persons, when they are afflicted and tossed to and fro, can be made to say almost anything. Others, when their souls are like perfectly placid waters, are just then in a condition to be navigated by the devil's vessel. Like a skilled metal worker, Satan knows exactly the temperature at which to work us to his purpose. Small pots come to a boil quickly, and so impatient men are soon in a passion. Larger vessels require more time and coal, but when they do boil, it is a boil not soon forgotten or abated.

Like a fisherman, the enemy watches his fish, adapts his bait to his prey, and knows in what seasons the fish are most likely to bite. This hunter of souls comes upon us unawares, and often we are overtaken in a fault or caught in a trap through lack of vigilance. To quote Thomas Spencer:

> Satan sets before us such objects of temptation as are most agreeable to our natures, that so he may the sooner draw us into his net; he sails with every wind, and blows us that way which we incline ourselves through the weakness of nature. Is our knowledge in matters of faith deficient? He tempts us to error. Is our conscience tender? He tempts us to scrupulosity, and too much preciseness. Hath our conscience, like the ecliptic line, some latitude? He tempts us to carnal liberty. Are we bold spirited? He tempts us to presumption. Are we timorous and distrustful? He tempts us to desperation. Are we of a flexible disposition? He tempts us to inconstancy. Are we stiff? He labors to make obstinate heretics, schismatics or rebels of us. Are we of an austere temper? He tempts us to cruelty. Are we soft and mild? He tempts us to indulgence and foolish pity. Are we hot in matters of religion? He tempts us to blind zeal and superstition. Are we cold? He tempts us to Laodicean lukewarmness. Thus doth he lay his traps, that one way or other, he may ensnare us.

Satan takes care to consider *our relationships*. While some people are most easily tempted when they are alone, most are more likely to sin when in a group. Among certain people, I would never be led into sin; with another group I dare not venture. There are certain settings where we are so inclined the same way as the group that we immediately feel our besetting sin set in motion. We know a certain brother who carries our own weakness, and be assured that between the two of us we will invent an evil report of the Promised Land. Satan knows to overtake us in a place where we lie open to his attacks; he will pounce, swoop like a bird of prey from the sky, where he has been watching for the time of vulnerability.

How, too, Satan will consider *our condition in the world!* As the sportsman has a gun for wild birds and another for deer, so Satan has a different temptation for various orders of men. He knows just where to strike, and our position, our capabilities, our education, our standing in society, our vocation, may all be doors through which he may attack us. You who have no vocation or work at all are in peculiar peril—I wonder the devil does not swallow you outright. The most likely man to go to hell is the man who has nothing to do on earth. I say that seriously. I would seek employment at once for fear I should be carried off, body and soul, by the evil one. Idle people tempt the devil to tempt them. Let us keep our minds occupied, for, if not, we make room for the devil. Work will not make us gracious, but the lack of it may make us vicious.

Satan, when he makes his investigation, notices all *the objects of our affection.* I doubt not that when he went around Job's house, he observed it as carefully as thieves do a jeweler's premises. When the devil went round, jotting down in his mind all Job's possessions, he thought, "There are the camels and the oxen, the asses, and the servants—yes, I can use all these very admirably. Then there are the daughters and sons who go feasting—I know where to catch them. And if I can just blow the house down, that will afflict the father's mind most severely, for he will say, 'O that they had died when they were praying rather than when they had been feasting and drinking wine.' I dare say I shall need his wife as well." Nobody could have done what Job's wife did—none of the servants could have said that sad sentence so stingingly: "Curse God, and die" (Job 2:9). Satan attacked Job's affections but did not succeed; Job's strength was in God. Perhaps the evil one had even inspected Job's feelings and selected the form of bodily affliction that he knew to be most dreaded.

Satan knows quite as much in regard to you. You have a child whom you adore. "Ah," says Satan, "there is a place for my wounding him." Even your spouse may be made a quiver in which hell's arrows shall be stored till the time comes. Our habits, our joys, our sorrows, our pleasures, our public positions, all may be weapons of attack by this desperate foe. We have snares everywhere: in our homes, at our work, and in the street. We find temptations in the house of God as well as in the world, traps in our high estate and deadly poisons in our abasement. We must not expect to be rid of temptations till we have crossed the Jordan, and then, thank God, we are beyond gunshot of the enemy. The last howling of the dog of hell will be heard as we descend into the chill waters of the black stream, but when we hear the hallelujah of the glorified, we shall have finished with the black prince forever and ever.

The Higher Consideration That Overrode His Consideration

In times of war, it is very common to countermine the enemy's mines. This is just what God does. Satan is mining, and he thinks to light the fuse and blow up God's building, but all the while God is undermining him and blows up Satan's mine before Satan can do any mischief. The devil is the greatest of all fools. He has more knowledge but less wisdom than any other creature. His subtlety is not wisdom, but only another shape of folly. All the while that Satan tempted Job, he did not know that he was answering God's purpose, for God was considering the whole of it and holding the enemy as a man holds a horse by its bridle. *The Lord had considered exactly how far He would let Satan go.* He did not at first permit Satan to touch Job's flesh—perhaps that was more than Job at that time could bear. The God who knows just how far to let the enemy go will say to him, "This far, and no farther." By degrees he became accustomed to his poverty; in fact, the trial had lost all its sting the moment Job said, "The LORD gave, and the LORD hath taken away." That enemy was slain—nay, it was buried, and this was the funeral message: "Blessed be the name of the Lord" (Job 1:21).

When the second trial came, the first trial had qualified Job to bear the second. The Lord who weighs mountains in scales had measured his servant's woe.

Did not the Lord also consider *how He would sustain His servant under the trial*? You do not know how blessedly your God poured the secret oil upon Job's fire of grace while the devil was throwing buckets of water on it. God says, "If Satan shall do much, I will do more; if he takes away much, I will give more; if he tempts him to curse, I will fill him so full of love for me that he shall bless me." Take those two truths and draw upon their strength—you will never be tempted without express license from the throne where Jesus pleads, and, on the other hand, when He permits it, He will with the temptation make a way of escape or give you grace to stand under it.

The Lord also considered *how to sanctify Job by this trial*. Job was "a perfect and an upright man" at first (Job 1:1), but I think there was just a sprinkle of self-righteousness in him, and his friends brought it out. Eliphaz and Zophar said such irritating things that poor Job could not help replying in strong terms about himself that were a little too much self-justification. Job was not proud, as some of us are, of very little—he had much to be proud of as the world values—but yet there was the tendency to be exalted with it. Though the devil did not know it, perhaps if he had left Job alone, that pride might have run to seed and Job might have sinned. But Satan was in such a hurry that he would not let the seed ripen, but he hastened to cut it up, and so was the Lord's tool to bring Job into a more humble and consequently a more safe and blessed state of mind.

Job was being *enabled to earn a greater reward*. God loves Job so much that He intends to give him twice the property. He intends to give him his children again. He means to make Job a more famous man than ever, a man whose name shall ring down the ages. Job is to be the man not of Uz but of the whole world. All men are to hear of Job's patience in the hour of trial. Who is to do this? Who is to fashion the trumpet of fame through which Job's name is to be blown? The devil goes to the forge and works away with all his might to make Job illustrious! Foolish devil! He is piling up a pedestal on which God will set his servant Job that he may be looked upon with wonder by all ages.

To conclude, *Job's afflictions and patience have been a lasting blessing to the church and have inflicted incredible disgrace upon Satan.* If you want to make the devil angry, throw the story of Job in his face. If you desire to have your own confidence sustained, may God the Holy Ghost lead you into the patience of Job. How many saints have been comforted in their distress by this history of patience! How many have been saved out of the jaw of the lion and from the paw of the bear by the dark experiences of the patriarch from Uz. O archfiend, how you are taken in your own net! You made a pit for Job and have fallen into it yourself. You are taken in your own craftiness. Jehovah has made fools of the wise and driven the diviners mad. Let us commit ourselves in faith to the care and keeping of God—come poverty, sickness, death, we will in all things through Jesus Christ's blood be conquerors, and by the power of His Spirit, we shall overcome at the last. Never stop trusting Jesus!

I look not upon the Scriptures as a harp that once was played by skillful fingers and is now hung up as a memorial upon the wall. No, they are an instrument of ten strings still in the minstrel's hand, still filling the temple of the Lord with divine music, which those who have ears to hear delight to listen to. Holy Scripture is an Aeolian harp, through which the blessed wind of the Spirit is always sweeping and creating mystic music such as no man's ears shall hear elsewhere, nor hear even there indeed, unless they have been opened by the healing touch of the Great Physician. The Holy Spirit is in the Word, and the Word is, therefore, living truth. Be assured of this, and because of it, take the Word as your chosen weapon of war.

Chapter Five

How to Use the Word of God

It is written—Matthew 4:4.

THOUGHTFUL MINDS ANXIOUSLY DESIRE some fixed point of belief. The old philosopher wanted a fulcrum for his lever and believed that if he could only obtain it he could move the world. The traveller at sea is delighted when he can plant his foot on solid ground again. We cannot rest till we have found something that is certain, sure, settled, decided, no longer to be questioned. Many a mind has peered into the hazy region of rationalism and seen nothing but perpetual mist and fog, and shivering with the cold chill of those arctic regions of skepticism, it is yearned for a clearer light, a warmer guide, a more tangible belief. This yearning has driven men into strange beliefs. Satan, seeing their ravenous hunger, has made men accept a stone for bread. Many have held, and still hold, that it is possible to find an infallible foundation in the Pope or other spiritual leaders. I do not wonder that they would rather have an infallible man than be altogether without a standard of truth, yet how any mind can by any possible contortion twist itself into a posture in which it will be capable of accepting such a belief is one of the mysteries of humanity. The notion of infallibility residing in mortal man is worthy of a madhouse and scarcely deserves to be seriously discussed.

Others, however, linger hopefully around the idea of an infallible church. They believe in the judgment of the general councils and hope there to find the rock of certainty. Apparently, this is easier, for in the multitude of counselors there is wisdom, but in reality it is quite as preposterous, for if you mass together a number of people, each one being fallible, it is clear that you are no nearer infallibility. It is as easy to believe that *one* man is inspired as that five hundred are so. The fact is that churches as well as individual men have made mistakes and have fallen into grievous errors both in doctrine and in practice. Look at the New Testament churches in Galatia, Corinth, Laodicea, Sardis, and so on. Even the apostles could blunder—and did blunder. They were infallible only when they wrote under the inspiration of the Holy Spirit and at no other time. Yet I do not marvel that in the sore distress to which the mind is often brought, it is found better to believe in an infallible church than to be left to mere reason, to be tossed to and fro, driven by ever changing winds over the awful leagues of questionings that are found in the restless ocean of unbelief.

But we have a surer word of testimony, a rock of truth upon which we rest, for our infallible standard lies in "It is written." The Bible, the whole Bible, and nothing but the Bible, is our standard. It is said that it is hard to understand, but it is not so to those who seek the guidance of the Spirit of God. The Bible contains great truths that are above our comprehension, placed there on purpose to let us see how shallow our finite minds are; but concerning vital and fundamental points, the Bible is not hard to understand, neither is there any excuse for the multitude of errors that people pretend to gather from it. A babe in grace taught by the Spirit of God may know the mind of the Lord concerning salvation and find its way to heaven by the guidance of the Word alone. The question is not whether the Bible is profound or simple. The Bible is the Word of God, and is pure, unerring truth. In it, and nowhere else, is infallibility.

This grand, infallible book is our sole court of appeal, the sword of the Spirit in the spiritual battles that await us. I zealously exhort you to take this part of the whole armor of God that you may be able to resist the great enemy of our souls. I commend this unfailing weapon "It is written" to the use of every believer by noting that *this is our Champion's own weapon*. Second, I note *to what uses He turned this weapon,* and third, we shall watch Him to see *how He handled it.*

It Is Our Champion's Weapon

When Jesus Christ was assailed by Satan in the wilderness, *He had a great choice of weapons* with which to fight Satan, *but He took none but this sword of the Spirit:* "It is written." Our Lord had only to pray to His Father and He would presently have sent Him twelve legions of angels against whose mighty rush the archfiend could not have stood for a single moment. If our Lord had but exercised His Godhead, a single word would have sent the tempter back to his infernal den. But instead of angelic or divine power, He used "It is written," thus teaching His church that she is never to call in the aid of force or use the carnal weapon but must trust alone in the omnipotence that dwells in the sure word of testimony. This is our battle-ax and weapon of war. A spiritual kingdom must be set up and supported by spiritual means only.

Our Lord might have defeated the tempter by unveiling His own glory. The brightness of the divine majesty was hidden within the humility of His manhood, and if He had lifted the veil for a moment, the fiend would have been as utterly confounded as bats and owls when the sun blazes in their faces. But Jesus chose to conceal His excellent majesty and defend Himself only with "It is written."

Our Master might also have assailed Satan with rhetoric and logic. Why did He not discuss the points with him as they arose? Here were three different propositions to be discussed, but our Lord confined Himself to one argument: "It is written." Now, if our Lord and Master selected this true Jerusalem blade of the Word of God, let us not hesitate for a moment but grasp and hold fast this one true weapon of the saints in all times. Cast away the wooden sword of carnal reasoning. Trust not in human eloquence but arm yourselves with the solemn declarations of God, who cannot lie, and you need not fear Satan and all his hosts. Jesus selected the best weapon. What was best for Him is best for you.

Our Lord *used this weapon at the outset of His career.* He had not yet come into the public ministry, but—if I may use the expression—while His young hand was yet untried in public warfare, He grasped at once the weapon ready forged for Him and boldly declared, "It is written." The Word of God is the child's weapon as truly as it is the defense of the strong man. If a believer were as tall as Goliath of Gath, he need have no better sword than this, and if he is only a child in the things of God, this sword will equally fit his hand and be equally effectual for offense or defense. What a mercy it is that you have not to argue but to believe, not to invent but to accept. You have only to open your Bible, find the text, and hurl it at Satan like a stone from David's sling, and you will win the battle. "It is written," and what is written is infallible; here is your strength in argument. God has said it; that is enough. O blessed sword and shield that the little child can use effectively, fit also for the illiterate and simple-minded, giving might and conquest to the weak.

Note next that *Christ used the Word when no man was near*. The value of Holy Scripture is not limited to public teaching or striving for the truth. The Word's still, small voice is equally powerful when the servant of the Lord is enduring personal trial in the lonely wilderness. The severest struggles of a true Christian are usually unknown to any but the Christian himself. We Christians meet the most subtle temptations in the place of prayer; in the deep recesses of our own spirit, we wrestle with principalities and powers. For these dread duels, "It is written" is the best sword and shield. Scripture to convince another man is good, but Scripture is most required to console, defend, and sanctify our own soul. We must know how to use the Bible alone and understand how to meet the subtlest of foes with it, for there is a real and personal devil, as most Christians know by experience, since they have stood foot to foot with him and have known his keen suggestions, horrible insinuations, blasphemous assertions, and fiendish accusations.

We Christians have been assailed by thoughts that came from a mind more vigorous, more experienced, and more subtle than our own, and against these thoughts the Word of God is our only defense. Many conflicts have taken place between God's servants and Satan that are more notable in the unpublished annals of sacred history that the Lord records than the bravest deeds of ancient heroes whom men praise in their national songs. There are victors who have fought with angels and prevailed, whose prowess even Lucifer must grimly admit. These all ascribe their victories to the grace that taught them how to use the infallible Word of the Lord.

Always have "It is written" ready by your side. Some, when a spiritual conflict begins, run to a friend for help. I do not condemn the practice, but it would be much better if they turned to the Lord and His sure promise. Some at the first onslaught are ready to give up all hope. Do not act in so dastardly a manner; seek grace to play the man. You must fight if you are to enter into heaven. Look to your weapon; it cannot bend or grow blunt; wield it boldly and plunge it into the heart of your enemy. "It is written" will cut through soul and spirit and wound the old dragon himself.

Note that *our Lord used this weapon under the most trying circumstances,* but He found it to be sufficient for His need. He was alone; no disciple was there to sympathize, but the Word was the man of His right hand, the Scriptures communed with Him. Jesus was hungry, since He had fasted forty days and nights, and oftentimes the spirits sink when the body lacks food. Yet "It is written" held the world of hunger at bay. The Word fed the Champion with such meat as not only removed all faintness but also made Him mighty in spirit. Jesus was placed by His adversary in a position of great danger, high on the pinnacle of the lofty house of the Lord, yet there He stood and needed no surer foothold than that which the promises of the Lord supplied Him. "It is written" enabled Him to look down from the dizzy height and baffle the tempter still. Our Lord was placed also where the kingdoms of the world were stretched beneath His feet, a matchless panorama that has often dazzled great men's eyes and driven men onward to destruction, but "It is written" swept aside the snares of ambition and laughed at the fascination of power. No change in His mode of warfare was required. The infallible Word availed in every position in which our Lord found Himself, and so shall it be with us.

Observe that our Savior *continued to use His one defense,* although His adversary frequently shifted his point of attack. Error has many forms; truth is one. The devil tempted Jesus to distrust, but that dart was caught upon the shield of "It is written, Man shall not live by bread alone, but by every word that proceedeth out of the mouth of God" (Matt. 4:4). The enemy aimed a blow at Jesus from the side of presumption, tempting Him to cast Himself down from the temple, but how terribly did that two-edged sword fall down upon the head of the fiend: "It is written again, Thou shalt not tempt the Lord thy God" (Matt. 4:7). The next impudent blow was levelled at our Lord with the intent of bringing Him to His knees. But "Fall down and worship me" was met and returned with crushing force by "It is written, Thou shalt worship the Lord thy God, and him only shalt thou serve" (Matt. 4:10). This smote Leviathan to the heart. This weapon is good at all points, good for defense and for attack, to guard our whole person or to strike through the joints and marrow of the foe. Like the seraph's sword at Eden's gate, it turns every way. You cannot be in a condition that the Word of God has not provided. The Word has as many faces and eyes as providence itself. You will find it unfailing in all periods of your life, in all circumstances, in all companies, in all trials, and under all difficulties. Were it fallible, it would be useless in emergencies, but its unerring truth renders it precious beyond all price to the soldiers of the cross.

I commend to you, then, the hiding of God's Word in your heart, the pondering of it in your minds. "Let the word of Christ dwell in you richly in all wisdom" (Col. 3:16). Be rooted and grounded and established in its teaching and saturated in its spirit. To me it is an intense joy to search diligently in my Father's book of grace which grows upon me daily. The Bible was written by inspiration in old times, but I have found while feeding upon it that not only *was* it inspired when written but it is so still. It is not a mere historic document. It is a letter fresh from the pen of God to me. It is not a flower dried and put by in the *hortus siccus*, with its beauty clouded and its perfume evaporated. It is a fresh blooming flower in God's garden, as fragrant and as fair as when God planted it.

I look not upon the Scriptures as a harp that once was played by skillful fingers and is now hung up as a memorial upon the wall. No, they are an instrument of ten strings still in the minstrel's hand, still filling the temple of the Lord with divine music, which those who have ears to hear delight to listen to. Holy Scripture is an Aeolian harp, through which the blessed wind of the Spirit is always sweeping and creating mystic music such as no man's ears shall hear elsewhere, nor hear even there indeed, unless they have been opened by the healing touch of the Great Physician. The Holy

Spirit is in the Word, and the Word is, therefore, living truth. Be assured of this, and because of it, take the Word as your chosen weapon of war.

How to Use This Word

Notice first that Jesus used the Word to *defend His sonship*. The fiend said, "If Thou be the Son of God," and Jesus replied, "It is written." That was the only answer He needed to give. Jesus did not call to mind evidences to prove His Sonship. He did not even mention that voice out of the excellent glory that had said, "This is My beloved Son." No, but "It is written."

I do not doubt but that you have been already subjected to the infernal "if." How glibly it comes from Satan's lip. It is his darling word, the favorite arrow of his quiver. Satan is the prince of skeptics, who worship him while he laughs in his sleeve at them, for he believes and trembles. One of his greatest works of mischief is to make men doubt. "If"—with that sneer he whispers this already in the ear. Never let Satan get you away from the solid ground of the Word of God. If he once gets you to think that the fact of Christ being the Savior of sinners can only be proved by what you can see within yourself, he will plunge you into despair.

The reason that I am to believe in Jesus lies in Jesus and not in me. I am not to say, "I believe in the Lord Jesus because I feel so happy," for within half an hour I may feel miserable; but I believe in Christ because it is written, "Believe on the Lord Jesus Christ, and thou shalt be saved" (Acts 16:31). I believe in the salvation provided by Jesus Christ not because it always agrees with my reason or suits my frame of mind but because it is written, "He that believeth on him is not condemned" (John 3:18). Nothing can alter this truth; it stands and must stand forever. Believer, abide by it, come what may. Satan will say, "You know there are many evidences; show me one." Tell him to mind his own business. He will say, "You know how imperfectly you have behaved, even since conversion." Tell him that he is not so wonderfully perfect that he can afford to find fault with you. If he says, "Ah, but if you were really a changed character you would not have those thoughts or feelings," argue not at all with him but dwell upon the fact that it is written, "Jesus Christ came into the world to save sinners" (1 Tim. 1:15).

"It is written." Stand upon it, and if the devil were fifty devils in one, he could not overcome you. On the other hand, if you leave "It is written," Satan knows more about reasoning than you do. He is far older, has studied mankind very thoroughly, and knows all our weak points. Therefore, the contest will be an unequal one. Do not argue with him but wave in his face the banner of God's Word. Satan cannot endure the infallible truth, for it is death to the falsehood of which he is the father.

Our Lord next used the Scripture *to defeat temptation*. He was tempted to distrust. There lay stones at His feet, there was no bread, and He was hungry. Distrust said, "God has left you; you will starve; therefore, stop being a servant, become a master, and command that these stones be made bread." Jesus, however, met the temptation confidently trusting God's Word. If you are placed by providence where you think you will be in need and are afraid that God will not provide for you, the dark suggestion will arise, "Whatever it takes, I must find a way to put myself in comfortable circumstances." True, the action would be wrong, but many do it, and therefore Satan whispers, "Necessity has no law; take the opportunity now before you." In such an hour, foil the enemy with "It is written, 'Trust in the LORD, and do good; so shalt thou dwell in the land, and verily thou shalt be fed' " (Ps. 37:3). In that way only can you safely meet the temptation to distrust.

Then Satan tempted the Lord to presumption. "If thou be the Son of God, cast thyself down," said he (Matt. 4:6). But Christ had a Scripture ready to parry his thrust. Many are tempted to presume. "You are one of God's elect, you cannot perish; you may therefore go into sin; you have no need to be careful, since you cannot fall finally and fatally"—so Satan whispers. If we are at any time tempted to yield to such specious pleadings, let us remember, it is written, "Watch and pray, that ye enter not into temptation" (Matt. 26:41). It is written, "Keep thine heart with all diligence; for out of it are the issues of life" (Prov. 4:23). It is written, "Be ye therefore perfect, even as your Father which is in heaven is perfect" (Matt. 5:48). Begone, Satan. We dare not sin because of the mercy of God. That were indeed a diabolical return for His goodness. We abhor the idea of sinning that grace might abound.

Then will Satan attack us with the temptation to be traitors to our God by worshipping other gods. "Worship me," says he, "and your reward will be great." He sets before us some earthly object that he would have us idolize, some selfish aim that he would have us pursue. At that time, our only defense is the sure word, It is written, "Thou shalt love the Lord thy God with all thy heart, with all thy soul, and with all thy mind, and with all thy strength" (Mark 12:30). "Ye are not your own, ye are bought with a price" (1 Cor. 6:20). "Present your bodies a living sacrifice, holy, acceptable unto God, which is your reasonable service" (Rom. 12:1). "Little children, keep yourselves from idols" (1 John 5:21). Quoting such words as those with all our hearts, we shall not fall. We must keep from sin. If Christ has indeed saved us from sin, we cannot bear the thought of falling into it. Those who take delight in sin are not the children of God. If you are a child of God, you hate it with a perfect hatred, and your very soul loathes it. To keep you from sin, arm yourselves with this most holy and pure Word of God which shall cleanse your way and make your heart obedient to the voice of the thrice-holy God.

Next our Lord used the Word as *a direction to His way*. This is a very important point. Too many direct their way by what they call providences. They do wrong things and they say, "It seemed such a providence." I wonder whether Jonah, when he went down to Joppa to flee to Tarshish, considered it a providence that a ship was about to sail. If so, he was like too many nowadays who seek to lay their guilt upon God by declaring that they felt bound to act as they did, for providence suggested it. Our Lord was not guided as to what He should do by the circumstances around Him. Anyone but our Lord would have obeyed the tempter and felt it was providence to turn the stones into bread. It was a providence, but it was a testing providence. When you are tempted to do wrong to relieve your necessities, say to yourself, "This providence is testing me but by no means indicates to me what I ought to do, for my rule is, 'It is written.' " If you make apparent providence your guide, you will make a thousand mistakes, but if you follow "It is written," your steps will be wisely ordered.

Nor are we to make our special gifts and special privileges our guide. Christ is on the pinnacle of the temple, and it is possible that if He had chosen to cast Himself down He could have done so safely, but He did not make His special privileges a reason for presumption. While it is true that the saints are kept by the power of God, I am not to presume upon a doctrine; I am to obey the precept. For a man to say, "I am a child of God, I am safe, and therefore I live as I want," would be to prove that he is no child of God at all, for the children of God do not turn the grace of God into licentiousness. That can only be the devil's logic.

Satan tried to make his own personal advantage our Lord's guide. "All these things will I give thee," said he, but Christ did not order His acts for His own personal advantage but replied, "It is written." Well might He have said, "If I fall down and perform this small act, all the kingdoms of the earth will be Mine! There are all those poor oppressed slaves; I could set them free. The hungry and the thirsty, I would supply their needs. Indeed, that is the very thing I am about to die for, and if it is to be done so easily by bowing the knee to this spirit, why not do it?" Far, far removed was our Lord from the wicked spirit of compromise. Though the whole world would be at His disposal, He would not compromise. "It is written" was His guide, not His usefulness or personal advantage.

Believer, it will sometimes happen that to do the right thing will appear to be most disastrous. It will shipwreck your fortune and bring you into trouble, but I charge you do the right thing at any cost. Instead of your being honored and respected and accounted a leader in the church, you may be regarded as eccentric if you speak straight out; but speak straight out and never mind what comes of it. You and I have nothing to do with what becomes of us or our reputations or with what becomes of the world or of heaven itself. Our one business is to do our Father's will. "It is written" is to be our rule. With dogged obstinacy as men call it, but with resolute consecration as God esteems it, through the mire and through the slough, through the flood and through the flame, follow Jesus and the Word infallible.

Note further that our Lord used "It is written" for *maintaining His own Spirit.* I love to think of the calmness of Christ. Christ is not the least flurried. He is hungry, and He is told to create bread, and He answers, "It is written." He is lifted to the temple's summit, but He says, "It is written" just as calmly as you and I might do sitting in an easy chair. There He is with the whole world beneath

His feet, gazing on its splendor, but He is not dazzled. "It is written" is still His quiet answer. Nothing makes a man self-contained, cool, and equal to every emergency like always falling back upon the infallible Book and remembering the declaration of Jehovah, who cannot lie.

The last thought on this point is that our Lord teaches us that the use of Scripture is *to vanquish the enemy and chase him away.* "Go," said He to the fiend, "for it is written." You too shall chase away temptation if you keep firmly to this: "God said it, God promised it; God cannot lie, whose very word of grace is strong as that which built the skies."

How Christ Handled the Word

How are we to handle this sword of "It is written"? First, *with deepest reverence.* Let every word that God has spoken be law and gospel to you. Never trifle with it; never try to evade its force or change its meaning. God speaks to you in this book as much as if He came to the top of Sinai and lifted up His voice with thunder. I like to open the Bible and pray, "Lord God, let the words leap off the page into my soul; make them vivid, powerful, and fresh to my heart." Our Lord Himself felt the power of the Word. It was not so much the devil who felt the power of "It is written" as Christ Himself. The manhood of Christ felt an awe of the Word of God, and so the Word became a power to Christ. To trifle with Scripture is to deprive yourself of its aid. Reverence it, and look up to God with devout gratitude for having given it to you.

Next *have it always ready.* Our Lord as soon as He was assailed had His answer prepared: "It is written." Have the Scriptures at your fingertips. Better still, have them in the center of your heart. It is a good thing to store the memory with many passages of the Word—the very words themselves. Our Savior knew so much of Holy Scripture that out of one single book—the book of Deuteronomy—He obtained all the texts with which He fought the wilderness battle. He had a wider range, for the Old Testament was before Him, but He kept to one book, as if to let Satan know that He was not short of ammunition. If the devil chose to continue the temptation, the Lord had abundant defense in reserve. "It is written" is an armory wherein hang a thousand bucklers, all shields of mighty men. It is not merely one but a thousand, nay, ten thousand weapons of war. It has texts of every kind, suitable for our aid in every emergency and effectual for repelling every attack. Study the Word of God and have it ready at your side when the father of lies approaches.

Endeavor also to *understand its meaning* and so to understand it that you can discern between its meaning and its perversion. Half the mischief in the world—and perhaps more—is done not by an ostensible lie but by a perverted truth. The devil, knowing this, takes a text of Scripture, clips it, adds to it, and attacks Christ with it. Our Lord did not therefore despise Scripture because the devil himself might quote it, but He answered him with a flaming text right in his face. He did not say, "The other is not written, you have altered it," but He gave him a taste of what "It is written" really was, and so confounded him. You can do the same. Search the Word, get the true taste of it in your mouth, and acquire discernment so that when you say, "It is written," you may not be making a mistake. Texts of Scripture out of context, twisted and perverted, are not "It is written," but the plain meaning of the Word should be known and understood. Read the Word and pray for the anointing of the Holy Spirit that you may know the Word's meaning, for so will you contend against the foe.

And *learn to appropriate Scripture to yourself.* One of the texts our Lord quoted He slightly altered. "Thou shalt not tempt the Lord thy God." The original text is, "Ye shall not tempt the Lord your God." But the singular lies in the plural, and it is always a blessed thing to be able to find it there. Learn so to use Scripture that you take home to yourself all its teaching, all its precepts, all its promises, all its doctrines, for bread on the table does not nourish; it is bread that you eat that will really sustain you.

When you have appropriated the texts to yourself, *stand by them whatever they may cost you.* If to give up the text would enable you to make stones into bread, do not give it up. If to reject the precept would enable you to fly through the air like a seraph, do not reject it. If to go against the Word of God would make you emperor of the entire world, do not accept the bribes. Go as far as the Bible but not an inch beyond it. Though Calvin should beckon you, and you esteem him, or Wesley should beckon, and you esteem him, keep to the Scripture only. If your minister should go astray, pray that he may be brought back again, but do not follow him. Though we or an angel from heaven preach any other gospel than this book teaches you, do not give any heed to us—no, not for a single moment. Here is the only infallibility: the Holy Ghost's witness in this book.

Remember, lastly, that your Lord at this time was *filled with the Spirit*. Jesus being filled with the Spirit went to be tempted (Matt. 4:16–5:1). The Word of God apart from the Spirit of God will be of no use to you. If you cannot understand a book, do you know the best way to reach its meaning? Write the author and ask him what he meant. If you have a book to read and you have the author always accessible, you need not complain that you do not understand it. The Holy Spirit has come to abide with us forever. Search the Scriptures, but cry for the Spirit's light and live under His influence. So Jesus fought the old dragon, "being filled with the Spirit." He smote Leviathan through with this weapon because the Spirit of God was upon Him. Go with the Word of God like a two-edged sword in your hand, but before you enter the battlefield, pray the Holy Ghost to baptize you into Himself; so shall you overcome all your adversaries and triumph even to the end.

*N*otice the point of attack: it was our Lord's sonship. Satan knows that if he can make any of us doubt the Father's love, doubt our regeneration and adoption, he will have us very much in his power. How can I pray "Our Father which art in heaven" if I do not know Him to be my Father? If the dark suspicion crosses my mind that I am no child of His, I cannot say with the prodigal, "I will arise and go unto my father." Having a Father, I feel sure that He will pity my weaknesses, feel for my needs, forgive my wrongs, protect me in the hour of danger, and save me in the moment of peril. But if, if I have no Father in heaven, then, miserable orphan! what shall I do, where shall I flee? Standing on the pinnacle as God's child, I shall stand there erect, though every wind should seek to whirl me from my foothold. But if He is not my Father and I am upon a pinnacle, my destruction is inevitable. "If thou be the Son of God." Beware of unbelief; those who justify unbelief hold a candle to the devil. God is faithful: why should we doubt Him? God is true: how can we suppose that He will be false?

Chapter Six

Temptations on the Pinnacle

Then the devil taketh him up into the holy city, and setteth him on a pinnacle of the temple, and saith unto him, If thou be the Son of God, cast thyself down: for it is written, He shall give his angels charge concerning thee: and in their hands they shall bear thee up, lest at any time thou dash thy foot against a stone. Jesus said unto him, It is written again, Thou shalt not tempt the Lord thy God—Matthew 4:5–7.

THE CLEAREST AND MOST IMPORTANT exposition of the revelation of God in the inspired Book is the revelation of God in the renewed man. Every Christian will discover, in proportion to his advances in divine knowledge, that the very things that are written in these hallowed pages are written in his own experience. We never fully understand divine truth until we experience it. The diamond of divine promise never glistens so brightly as when it is placed in the setting of personal trial and experience, and the gold of sacred truth is not valued until it has been tried "so as by fire."

Holy Scripture is full of narratives of temptations. Expect, therefore, that your life will be as abundantly garnished with them as is a rose with thorns. Provision is made in the Word of God for the assaults of Satan from all directions and in all fashions. Believe, therefore, most confidently, that the wise provisions of forethought will be required in your life. You will have to do battle with those spiritual foes that have beset and buffeted other saints in days gone by, and you will be wise to array yourself in those pieces of heavenly armor that proved to be so great a safeguard to them in their seasons of warfare.

This remark—that the Word of God is written out again in the life of the believer—is emphatically true in that part of it that concerns the life of Jesus, for every Christian is the image of Christ in proportion as he is a Christian. In proportion as the Spirit sanctifies us—spirit, soul, and body—and makes us like the Master, we are conformed to Him, not only in the holiness and spirituality that sanctification produces but also in our experience of conflict, sorrow, agony, and triumph. In all points, Jesus was made like His brethren, and now it remains that in all things His brethren should be made like Him. The Savior's public life begins and ends with temptation. It commences in the wilderness in a close contest with satanic craft; it ends in Gethsemane in a dreadful affray with the powers of darkness. There are a few bright spots between, but the gloom of the desert deepens into the midnight darkness of the cross, as if to show that we also must begin with trial and can count upon ending with it. The victory of our Lord was won upon Golgotha in blood and wounds, amid the blasphemous exultation of His foes, and the victory of the believer will not be cheaply bought. Our crown is not to be won without wrestling and overcoming. We must fight if we would reign, and through the same conflicts that brought the Savior to His crown must we obtain the palm branch of everlasting victory.

The Temptation of Christ

The landscape is colored by the glass through which the observer looks, but still the landscape is really seen. And so in giving you much of that which I have myself been made to endure, I may color our Lord's trial, but you will see it nevertheless, and the Holy Spirit will show you what is really of Jesus and what is only mine. Our trials are sent us on purpose to make us comprehend our Lord's trials, and especially is it so with ministers of the gospel.

Martin Luther was a mighty master in the art of consolation because there was scarcely a temptation that he had not experienced. Melancthon bears witness of Luther that he was sometimes so tempted of the devil that he appeared to be at the point of death. The strength of Luther's life seemed to have dried up, and his soul was full of heaviness. After such seasons, Luther would so preach that his hearers thought that he was speaking concerning them alone and wondered where his knowledge was derived. He learned the art of spiritual navigation from having himself travelled upon deep waters of spiritual tribulation. Luther's remarks stand true, that prayer, meditation, and temptation are the three best instructors of the gospel minister, and since I have recently spent a good deal of time in the last school, I cannot do other than use what I have learned.

I first call attention to *the place of this temptation*. "Then the devil taketh him up into the holy city, and setteth him on a pinnacle of the temple." It was a *high* place and a *holy* place, hence a double danger. It was a *high* place: the temptation could not have acted upon the Savior had He been sitting in the desert or kneeling in the garden; but aloft, above the city, on the towering pinnacle, the foothold was slender, and the fall would have been terrible. Beneath Him lay a wondrous panorama—the courts of the Lord's house, the streets of the city, the towns and villages of Judea, and the broad acres of Immanuel's land. Little, however, would He care for all these, for His thoughts were concentrated upon the combat within, yet the widened prospect must have aided to the sense of elevation, and so have aided the temptation. One should not underestimate how hard it is to stand in high places. For instance, high places of importance in society and wealth bring temptations that positions of lowliness do not experience. I would be afraid to exchange my temptations with any other man, and yet I know my own to exceed my ability to overcome were it not for the grace of God and the promise, "My grace is sufficient for thee" (2 Cor. 12:9). It is hard to carry a full cup without spilling. When the cup is half full, you may carry it more carelessly without a slip, but when the golden chalice is full to the brim, beware, thou cupbearer of the King. You may leap like children at play, you may run where you will, but up along the narrow knifelike ridge, where awful precipices descend on either side, take care, O traveller, for one slip may be fatal. Look beneath, through the grim mist that hides the depths below, and be deeply grateful for the invisible and omnipotent hand that has sustained you until now.

The remarks to high places apply not merely to high places of wealth or influence or fame but also to places high for us, comparatively high places of enjoyment or satisfaction. Nor must I exclude holy places from the remarks. The mountain may be Tabor, but it is a mountain still. If you are called to the elevated position of one who dwells in rapt fellowship with Christ, there are temptations peculiar even to that happy state of mind. The pinnacle is none the less a pinnacle because it happens to be a pinnacle of the temple; it is even more dangerous. The place was not only high but also holy. Note how that is marked in the text. He takes Him to the *holy city* and to the pinnacle of the *temple*—two terms that might bring up vividly before the reader's mind the sanctity of the position.

To stand in a high place in God's house is very desirable and honorable, but it is both responsible and perilous. Let those beware whom God exalts in Israel. He of whom it is written that it were better for that man that he had never been born was an apostle. He who was the intimate friend of Christ is that man whose damnation surpasses all others in its flaming terrors. It is a very delightful thing to minister to a large congregation; it is wonderful to become a leader in the church; it is no small privilege to be permitted by the pen or by the tongue to edify multitudes of saints; but alas, the high places even of God's temple are dizzy places, and lofty positions in the church are sites where temptations attack us that would be unknown to us if in the humble obscurity of a retiring godliness we were to lie down in green pastures and feed beside the still waters. After all, if I might be allowed to envy anybody, it would be the singing Shepherd of John Bunyan's, as he feeds his flock in the valley:

> He that is down need fear no fall,
> He that is low no pride;
> He that is humble ever shall
> Have God to be his guide.

What do you think were the temptations that came upon the Savior on account of His position on the high and holy place? We frequently forget that the Savior was most truly man. He was divine without mitigation of royalty and splendor of Deity. But He was man, altogether such as we are, so that He felt as you and I would have felt in a similar condition. How then did He feel? Did He not tremble with fear of falling? I believe that the natural fear came over Him, as He stood there and looked down, that He would fall and that falling, He would stain the battlements of the consecrated place and crimson the house of God with His own blood.

Was He not a man—and what man would feel otherwise? It is natural that a shivering emotion of dread should creep over anyone standing in so lofty and unprotected a position. Now this is a temptation—a temptation to which God's servants who are put upon the pinnacle of the temple will find themselves frequently subject. But is it a fault to be afraid of falling? No, but there is something that grows out of the fear that is very faulty—namely, the temptation to do something desperate to escape from the position that is so full of peril. It is right for me to be afraid of falling into sin; it is not right for me either to mistrust God's grace that will sustain me or to run to foolish means to escape from the particular peril in which I happen to be involved. Jesus did not doubt His Father's care, but He did tremble because of the danger in which He was placed. He must have done so, because He was a man of like passions with ourselves.

May I picture you lifted up to such a position? Either in wealth, or in honor, or in communion, or in some way, you are lifted up into a sphere of danger, and you begin to say to yourself, "Suppose I fall! Suppose I should disgrace my profession and bring dishonor upon the cause of Christ!" I can understand that thought crossing your mind without any sin being involved in it, nay, with even a good resolve springing from it—namely, to walk humbly with your God. But I can suppose it to be the fulcrum upon which Satan may plant his lever and begin to work so as to bring you into a very sadly weakened and wretched state of mind. When I see others falling from their pinnacles, when I feel my own head grow dizzy, when I look down and see the ruin that must come upon every man who apostatizes from the faith, when I look up and see the holiness of God and then look down and feel the attractions of the world enticing and drawing me down to destruction, I tremble. If you are placed in such a position you *must* feel it.

This seems to me the reason that the devil put our Lord on the pinnacle of the temple. The first effort of the devil was to sap the foundations of the Savior's strength with *a doubt*. The devil whispers to Him, "*If—if* thou be the Son of God." Faith is the Christian's strength; he who doubts not staggers not. Unbelief is the source of our chief weakness. As soon as we begin to distrust, our feet begin to slide. Knowing this, Satan injects that cruel and wicked suspicion, "*If—if* thou be the Son of God."

Notice the point of attack: it was our Lord's sonship. Satan knows that if he can make any of us doubt the Father's love, doubt our regeneration and adoption, he will have us very much in his power. How can I pray "Our Father which art in heaven" if I do not know Him to be my Father? If the dark suspicion crosses my mind that I am no child of His, I cannot say with the prodigal, "I will arise and go unto my father" (Luke 15:18). Having a Father, I feel sure that He will pity my weaknesses, feel for my needs, forgive my wrongs, protect me in the hour of danger, and save me in the moment of peril. But if, *if* I have no Father in heaven, then, miserable orphan! what shall I do, where shall I flee? Standing on the pinnacle as God's child, I shall stand there erect, though every wind should seek to whirl me from my foothold. But if He is not my Father and I am upon a pinnacle, my destruction is inevitable. "If thou be the Son of God." Beware of unbelief; those who justify unbelief hold a candle to the devil. God is faithful: why should we doubt Him? God is true: how can we suppose that He will be false?

If, having nothing, I have cast myself at the foot of the cross; if, all guilty and defiled, I have seen in Jesus Christ all that my soul can want, then I am one with Jesus and a joint heir with Him. I must be the child of God because I am one with Christ Jesus, His only begotten and His well-beloved. Let me exhort you to seek after the full assurance of your sonship with God the Father. Give neither sleep to your eyes nor slumber to your eyelids unless you know that you are in the divine family. Remember that doubts here are perilous to the last degree, and most of all perilous to those who stand upon the pinnacle. To doubt in the valley brings sorrow, but to doubt on the mountain can be destructive. Thus, you see that the Savior was first assailed with a malicious and cruel insinuation of doubt.

The cunning tempter has paved the way for *the satanic suggestion*: "Cast thyself down." That advice looks like the most absurd thing that could be suggested. Jesus is afraid of falling and is therefore told to throw Himself down. If you do not understand this, it is because you are not acquainted with satanic methods. The human mind oscillates very strangely. Though at first it may be driven by main force from left to right, it naturally swings to the left again, returning by sheer necessity to the same point. There have been persons who have starved themselves to death from the fear of being poor and have brought on disease by fearing disease. Others have sought to destroy themselves when condemned because they dreaded being hanged. What escape from death suicide can offer is hard to say, but some have tried it. In a position where I cannot stand, the natural thing is to throw myself down directly. You are afraid as you stand on the brink of the cliff, afraid that you may fall over, and all the while a mad inclination to fall over may steal over you. It is strange, but then we are strange creatures. Though this looks like a very unlikely temptation, it is not unnatural. It is consistent with the well-known laws of consciousness that we are often tempted to do the very thing that we are afraid of doing and to do it to escape from it. Cast thyself down, lest you should fall.

Let me show you the shapes in which this temptation has come to some of us. The minister is placed in a position where his labors and troubles are incessant. He is afraid with so much to do and such delicate things to handle that he may make a mistake and injure the church that he designs to bless. The dark suggestion crosses his mind, "Give it up, leave the work," that is to say, do the worst mischief that you can to the church to prevent your doing the church any mischief! The same thing happens in business: you have striven to pay every man his own, to provide things honest in the sight of all men, but things are, at this moment, very unprofitable. Satan has whispered to many, "Get out of it! Go somewhere else! Leave it and flee the bills."

Take another case. You are a Christian, but you live in a family where there are manifold hindrances to your godliness. You can hardly get alone to pray. You certainly never hear a good word from loved ones. You have been fighting for God until now, and the enemy is at this moment saying, "Do not try it any longer; renounce your profession, give it up; go back to the world again;"

that is to say, so that you may not dishonor Christ, you are tempted to dishonor Him.

It is strange, but strangely true! I thank God for the story of Jonah. That miserable, morose old prophet has ever been a warning to some of us. God said to Jonah, "Go to Ninevah and preach!" "No," thought Jonah, "I cannot do that. How can I go and preach to such a city? It will not be to my honor." So away he goes to Tarshish. He little knew that in trying to avoid trouble he was running into it. So it is also with you. You want to go to Tarshish to get away from Ninevah; that is, you run into the depths of the sea to escape the rivers, you run into the fire to escape the frying pan. If you are passing through a terrible, severe, and fiery ordeal, I point you to the Savior standing on the pinnacle of the temple and bid you imitate Him in standing still fast and firm against the desperate foe. "That ye may be able to withstand in the evil day, and having done all, to stand" (Eph. 6:13).

The suggestion to cast Himself down was *backed up by a text of Scripture* (Ps. 91:11)—wicked advice sustained by a foolish argument. "Cast thyself down, because he has given his angels charge over thee, to keep thee." Notice he knocks out the words "in all thy ways," which limits the protection promised. The Lord never promises to keep us in ways of our own choosing. Every duty that is required of us and every path that is mapped out by Providence shall have divine protection accorded to its travellers, but if we go our own road, we have no promise that we will be cared for.

When the devil takes something away from a text, he generally puts something of his own in its place. He therefore added these words, "lest *at any time*." His object was to break down the text's hedges and to remove its landmarks. We have a promise that along the King's highway to heaven no lion shall be there, neither shall any ravenous beast go up thereon, but the redeemed shall be found there. But if I follow a path into the wilderness or go away into the jungle of my own superstition and folly, I cannot expect protection; and if I begin to travel *at any time*, choosing my own times instead of waiting for the pillar of cloud, I am not under the divine protection, nor can I expect it. Does the text as you find it in the ninety-first psalm give you any reason to believe that if you throw yourself down from the pinnacle, God would bring you to the bottom safely? Certainly not; a fair reading of it shows only that God will keep us in the path of duty.

It is a precious doctrine that the saints are safe, but it is a damnable inference from it that they may live as they please. It is a glorious truth that God will keep His people, but is an abominable falsehood that sin will do them no harm. Remember that God gives us liberty, not license, and while He gives protection, He will not allow presumption. If God sends me trouble, He will yield me deliverance from it, but if I make trouble myself, I must bear it. If Providence permits the devil to set me upon a pinnacle, even then God will help me, but if I throw myself down, then woe unto me, for I depart from the grace of God. Yet the temptation is not uncommon. Do such and such a thing, your eternal interests are safe; therefore shun God's service, throw up the reins, and let the horses go as they will, God will guide them; do not touch the tiller, the God of the wind will manage the vessel; do not put your shoulder to the wheel at all, but cry out to God to help you, and sit down and be lazy. That is the devil's talk, and our poor silly distracted minds too readily drink it in. But if God gives us grace, we shall say, "God helps those who help themselves; God works for those that work with Him, and in the name of God, I set up my banner; wherever He will call me I will go, though it be through floods and flames; and if He set me upon the pinnacle of the temple, I will do nothing but stand there till He takes me down, but as to throwing myself down to escape, O my Father, my God, help me to wrestle with this temptation and make me more than a conqueror through Your dear Son."

And what of *the answer that the Savior gave*? He said, "It is written, Thou shall not tempt the Lord thy God." Notice that Jesus met a promise misused with a precept properly applied. At that moment, the precept was worth more to Christ than the promise. There are certain people who love the promise part of God's Word but cannot bear the precept. There are those who when the minister preaches upon a sweet text are greatly delighted; that is savory meat such as their soul loves. But if the pastor expounds a precept of God's Word, they turn away and say, "He is a legalist."

It is not safe to pick and choose in the matters of divine truth. All hail, you fair promises! You meet me as the angels met Jacob at Mahanaim; but all hail, fair precepts! You meet me as Nathan met David and rebuke me for my sins. You also are my friends, and I salute you and am glad to bear you company. We must have the promises, precepts, exhortations, and rebukes. The compound of the Scripture—like the powders of the merchants for sweetness and excellence—must not be injured by being robbed of one single ingredient. Love the precept. Be of the mind of David who wrote the whole of Psalm 119, not so much in praise of the promise as in praise of the statutes and the laws of God. Sometimes a precept is the necessary counteracting principle to guard us from the perversion of the promise. Promises alone are like candies given to children which when too profusely eaten bring on sickness, but the precept comes as a healthy medicine so that you may feed upon the promise without injury.

Are you tempted to shun God's service and love? Hear this: "thou shalt not tempt the Lord thy God." You do so, you do tempt God; you tempt Him to sanction your sin when you use wrong means to escape from danger. A Christian who stoops to falsify records to escape his present financial dilemma is tempting God, for he asks God to help him and then uses evil tools to effect escape. Will you tempt God to assist you in defrauding your neighbor? Dare you ask God to aid you in doing what is not strictly upright? Do not dare to do this. "Thou shalt not tempt the Lord thy God." The Christian worker who dares to run away from work and says, "God will take care of me"—what is he doing? He is asking God one of two things: either to destroy him, which God will not do, for He is a faithful God, or to uphold and comfort him when he is not in the path of duty, which it would be wrong for God to do, since He cannot give the sweetness of His comfort and the joy of His countenance to a man who would thereby be encouraged in sin.

Beware of provoking God to jealousy. Though there are great depths beneath you, you cannot fall while He upholds. Though others are dashed in pieces and you can hear the crash of their fall, yet He upholds the righteous. Though you feel like panicking and are ready to slip from your foothold, yet the eternal God is your refuge, and underneath you are the everlasting arms. Your extremity of weakness shall be the opportunity of His power, and when you fall back faint and ready to die, it is then that the angelic wings shall be of service, and the cherub-helpers shall bear you up in their arms lest you dash your foot against a stone. Only be very courageous and confident and say to the fiend of hell, "Get thee hence, for the God who allowed me to be placed here never did forsake me and never will, and while He is for me, I will not fear." What may occur is no business of mine; it rests with Him. It is mine to stand in the path of duty, for thus I shall be in the place of safety.

Encouragements to Stand

The first encouragement is this. It is a simple thought, but it has tasted like nectar to my weary heart. *Jesus was tempted as I am.* You have heard that truth a thousand times, but have you grasped it? Jesus was not exempted from any of the temptations that occur to us. He was tempted to the very same sins into which we fall. Do not dissociate Jesus from yourself. It is a dark room that you are going through, but Jesus went through it before. It is a sharp fight that you are waging, but Jesus has stood foot to foot with the same enemy. It was a great encouragement to the Macedonians in their weary marches when they saw Alexander toiling always with them. They won their battles, and they drove the Persians before them as lions drive a herd of sheep, principally through the personal prowess of Alexander. First to leap the ditch, first to cross the river or scale the rampart, always adventuring himself for death or glory, every man grew into a hero at the sight of the hero. Let it be so with followers of Jesus. Jesus stays not in the pavilion when His children are in conflict, but He buckles on His armor and puts on His helmet, and above the cry of them that contend for mastery may be heard His cry, "I have trodden down strength." Jesus goes so far into the fight that He advances beyond the front rank and can say, "I have trodden the winepress *alone;* and of the people there was none with me" (Isa. 63:3). Let us be of good cheer: Christ has trodden the way before us, and the blood-bedabbled footsteps of the King of glory may be seen along the road that we traverse at this hour.

There is something sweeter yet, *Jesus was tempted but Jesus never sinned.* Then, my soul, it is not needful for you to sin, for Jesus was a man, and if one man endured these temptations and sinned not, by the same grace, another may do so. Keep in mind that to be tempted is not to sin. Often, God's servants in their worst and bitterest temptations are to a great extent free from sin and are to be pitied—not to be blamed. John Bunyan has a famous picture of Christian going through the Valley of the Shadow of Death when the fiends whispered temptations in his ears. "So," said he, "I did verily think that these were in my own heart," whereas they were only temptations of the devil and not his own, and whereas he hated them, there was no sin in them—to him, I mean. In this you may be encouraged, that you may go through the fiercest possible temptation heated seven times hotter, like Nebuchadnezzar's furnace, and yet the fire may not injure you, but you may come out with not so much as the smell of fire upon you, though you have walked in the midst of the glowing coals.

The third thing that comforts us is that *not only did Jesus not fall, but He gloriously triumphed.* Satan received a desperate fall and a deep discouragement as the result of this conflict, and as Jesus overcame, so may we. Jesus is the representative man for His people; the head has triumphed, and the members shared in the victory. While a man's head is above water you cannot drown his body. The head is above the great water of temptation, and we, who are the lower members, are not drowned, nor shall we be. We shall wade through the swelling current and land safely upon Canaan's side. "They feared as they entered into the cloud" (Luke 9:34), it is said of the disciples on the Mount, but their Master was with them there, and therefore their fears were frivolous. We, too, are fearing because we have entered the cloud or are in the midst of it, but our fears are needless and vain, for Christ is with us, armed for our defense. Our place of safety is the bosom of the Savior. Perhaps we are tempted just now to drive us nearer to Him. Blessed be any wind that blows me into the port of my Savior's love! Happy, happy, happy wounds that make me seek the beloved Physician, yea, blessed death, which with black wings shall bear me up to my Savior's throne. Anything is good that brings us to Christ; anything is mischievous that parts us from Him. Come, you who are tempted, come to your tempted Savior; come, you cast down and troubled, however much dismayed, come to Him. He forgets not the temptations through which He passed, and He is ready to help you in the same.

There is no believer in Christ, no follower of that which is true and lovely and of good repute, who will not find himself, at some season or other, attacked by this foul fiend and the legions enlisted in his service. Behold your adversary. Though you cannot see his face and detect his form, believe that such a foe withstands you. He is not a myth, nor a dream, nor a superstitious imagination. He is as real a being as ourselves. Though a spirit, he has as much real power over hearts as we have over the hearts of others, nay, in many cases far more. This is no vision of the night, no phantom of a disordered brain. That wicked one is as sternly real this day as when Christ met him in deadly conflict in the wilderness of temptation. Believers now have to fight with Apollyon in the Valley of Humiliation. Against this prince of darkness we declare the warning of the apostle, "Whom resist stedfast in the faith."

Chapter Seven

The Roaring Lion

Be sober, be vigilant; because your adversary the devil, as a roaring lion, walketh about, seeking whom he may devour: whom resist stedfast in the faith, knowing that the same afflictions are accomplished in your brethren that are in the world—1 Peter 5:8–9.

SATAN, WHO IS CALLED by various names in Scripture that are all descriptive of his character, was once an angel of God, perhaps one of the chief among the fiery ones:

Foremost of the sons of light,
Midst the bright ones doubly bright.

Sin, all-destroying sin, which has made an Aceldama out of Eden, soon found inhabitants for hell in heaven itself, plucking one of the brightest stars of the morning from its sphere and quenching it in blackest night. From that moment, this evil spirit, despairing of all restoration to his former glories and happiness, has sworn perpetual hostility against the God of heaven. He has had the audacity to openly attack the Creator in all His works. He stained creation. He pulled down man from the throne of glory and rolled him in the mire of depravity. With the trail of the serpent, he despoiled all Eden's beauty and left it a waste that brings forth thorns and briers, a land that must be tilled with the sweat of one's face. Not content with that, inasmuch as he had spoiled the first creation, he has incessantly attempted to despoil the second. Man, once made in the image of God, he soon ruined. Now he uses all his devices, all his craft, all the power of his skill, and all the venom of his malice to destroy twice-born man, created in the image of Christ Jesus. With ceaseless toil and untiring patience, he is ever occupied in endeavoring to crush the seed of the woman.

There is no believer in Christ, no follower of that which is true and lovely and of good repute, who will not find himself, at some season or other, attacked by this foul fiend and the legions enlisted in his service. Behold your adversary. Though you cannot see his face and detect his form, believe that such a foe withstands you. He is not a myth, nor a dream, nor a superstitious imagination. He is as real a being as ourselves. Though a spirit, he has as much real power over hearts as we have over the hearts of others, nay, in many cases far more. This is no vision of the night, no phantom of a disordered brain. That wicked one is as sternly real this day as when Christ met him in deadly conflict in the wilderness of temptation. Believers now have to fight with Apollyon in the Valley of Humiliation. Against this prince of darkness we declare the warning of the apostle, "Whom resist stedfast in the faith."

I shall approach this from four points. First of all, *Satan's incessant activity*—"He walketh about as a roaring lion, seeking whom he may devour"; second, we will dwell *upon his terrible roarings*; third, *upon his ultimate aim*, seeking to devour God's people; and last, let us take up the exhortation of Peter and *show how Satan is to be overcome*.

Satan's Perpetual Activity

Only God can be omnipresent; hence, Satan can be in only one place at one time. Yet, if you consider how much trouble he does, you will easily gather that he must have an awful degree of activity. He is here and there and everywhere, tempting us here, scattering his temptations in countries afar, hurrying across the sea, or speeding over the land. We have no means of ascertaining his means of flight, but we may easily infer from his being so constantly in all places that he must travel with inconceivable velocity. He has, besides, a host of fallen spirits who fell with him. This great dragon drew with his tail the third part of the stars of heaven—and these are ready to execute his will and obey his commands, if not with the same potency and force that belongs by hereditary right to their great leader, still with something of his spirit, malice, and cunning.

How active he must be! We know *that he is to be found in every place!* Enter the most hallowed sanctuary, and you will find him there. Go to Wall Street, and you will lack no signs of his being present there. Retire into the quietude of the family circle, and you will soon detect in bickerings and jealousies that Satan has scattered handfuls of evil seed there. No less in the deep solitude of the hermit's cave might you find the tracks of his cloven foot. He is found in the clashing of swords, in the tyrant's heart, and even in the enmity that is excited in the breasts of those who are oppressed. Travel into the wilds where no Christian missionary ever trod, and you will find that Satan has penetrated the far interior and tutored the barbarian. Satan is the prince of the power of the air. Wherever the breath of life is inhaled, the poisonous atmosphere of temptation is a thing familiar.

Remember that as he is found in all places, so *you have often found him wherever you go.* You have sought to serve God in your daily business, but strong temptations, furious thoughts of evil, have followed you there. You have come home almost brokenhearted with your slips, intending to magnify your Master there, but your easily besetting sin overturned you, and Satan exalted at your fall. You have said, "I will go to bed," but in your tossings at midnight you have found him there. You have risen and said, "I will pray," but who among us has not met the foul fiend even there in solitary conflict? When we wished to be wrestling with the Angel of God, we have had to contend with the fiend of hell. Look at the marks of sin in your life and on some, not only marks of sin but also marks of Satan's presence. Satan is not in all sin; we sin of ourselves. We must not lay too much upon Satan's shoulders. Sin grows in our hearts without any sowing, just as thorns and thistles will grow in fallow furrows. Still, there are times when Satan himself must have been present, and you have had to know it and feel it. How often he has marred and stained the best performance of our most willing hands.

We must observe also *how ready Satan is to vent his spite against us in all frames of heart*. When we are depressed in spirit, that old coward Satan is sure to attack us. I have always noted that he prefers to attack some of us when we are in a low and weak state rather than at any other time. Oh, how temptation has staggered us when we have been sick! On the other hand, if we are joyous and triumphant and are something in the frame of mind that David was when he danced before the ark, then Satan knows how to set his traps by tempting us to presumption—"My mountain standeth firm, I shall never be moved"—or else to carnal security—"Soul, take thine ease, thou hast much goods laid up for many years"— or to self-righteousness—"My own power and goodness exalted me." Or he will even attempt to poison joys with evil forebodings. "Ah!" says he. "This is too good to hold; you will soon be cast down, and all these fine plumes shall be trodden like the mire of the streets." He well knows how, in every frame of mind, to make our condition serve his devouring purposes. He will follow you when your soul is all but despairing and whisper, "God hath forsaken thee, and given thee over to the will of thine enemies." And he will track your upward course, riding as it were on cherubs' wings, when you tread the starry pathway of communion. On the temple's pinnacle, he will tempt you, saying, "Cast thyself down"; and on the mountain's peak, he will attack you with, "Bow down and worship me."

And remember how well he knows *how to turn all the events of providence against us*. Here comes Esau, hungry with hunting; there is a meal of pottage ready, that he may be tempted to sell his birthright. Here is Noah, glad to escape from his long confinement in the ark; he is merry, and there is the wine cup ready for him that he may drink. Here is Peter; his faith is low, but his presumption is high; there is a maiden ready to say, "This fellow was also with Jesus of Nazareth" (Matt. 26:71). There is Judas, and there are thirty pieces of silver in the priestly hand to tempt him. No lack of means! If there is a Jonah, wishing to go to Tarshish rather than Ninevah, there is a ship ready. Satan has his providences as if to counterfeit the providence of God. At least, he knows how to use God's providence to serve his own ends.

One of the great mercies God bestows upon us is His not permitting our inclinations and opportunities to meet. Have you not sometimes noticed that when you have had the inclination to a sin, there has been no opportunity, and when the opportunity has presented itself, you have had no inclination toward it. Satan's principal aim with believers is to bring their desires and his temptations together—to get their souls into a dry, seared state and then to strike the match and make them burn. Satan is so crafty and wily with all the experience of these many centuries that man is no match for him. Did he not drag down the wise man Solomon, whose wisdom was more excellent than any of the sons of men? Did he not cast down the strong man Samson, who could slay a thousand Philistines but could not resist Delilah? Did he not bring down even the man after God's own heart by a most sorrowful fault? Let us seriously remember that we have never met an upright man over whom Satan has not in some degree triumphed.

Satan's terrible activity follows us into all places. Of course, there are skeptics who will not believe in the existence of this evil spirit. Too generally I have noticed that when a man has no devil, he has no God. Usually when a man does not believe there is a devil, it is because he never experiences Satan's attacks, and probably never will. But I say this, if a man has ever met Satan, as John Bunyan describes Christian meeting Apollyon in the Valley of Humiliation, he will have no doubt of the existence of a devil. When I have stood foot to foot with that arch-tempter in some dire hour of conflict, I could no more doubt his being there struggling and wrestling with my soul than a soldier could doubt that there must have been an antagonist to inflict his bleeding wounds. Experience will be to man, after all, the best proof of this, and we cannot expect that those who have never known the joys of the Holy Spirit will know much about the attacks of Satan, nor that those who doubt that there is a God can ever be much tormented with the devil. "Oh!" Satan says. "Let them alone, they will fall into the ditch by themselves; there is no need that I should go abroad after them."

Satan's Roarings

The destroyer has many methods of mischief. Here in the text he is compared to a *roaring* lion. In some passages of Scripture he is compared to a fowler. Now a fowler makes no noise; it would altogether defeat his end if he were to frighten the birds. But as quietly as possible he sets his lure, and with sweet notes he seeks to enchant his victim till it is taken in the trap. That is quite a different thing from the roaring lion. In another passage it is said that he knows how to transform himself into an angel of light; and then, plausibly and smoothly, he teaches false doctrine and error and all the time appears to have a holy zeal for truth and the most earnest love for that which is delicate and lovely and of good repute. We have plenty of examples of writers who hate true Christianity as much as the devil hates virtue, and you find them writing very pious lamentations over the presumed follies of some honest preacher. Of all devils, the most devilish is the saintly hypocrite loving sin and yet pleading against it in order to promote it. In this text, however, he is not an angel of light but a roaring lion. I think it was Rutherford who said that he liked the devil best in this shape. I remember in one of his letters he thanks God that He had given him a *roaring* devil to deal with. Now the peculiar temptation that is intended under the metaphor is that of a lion that roars till he startles the forests and shakes the hills.

These roarings of Satan are threefold. Perhaps Peter here alluded *to the roaring of persecution.* How Satan roared with persecutions in Peter's day! He roared, and roared, and roared again, till none but stout hearts dared to show themselves valiant for Christ. There were the underground prisons where fresh air never chased away the noxious smell and pestilential vapor. There were racks and gibbets. There were the sword for beheading and the stake for burning. There was dragging at the heels of the wild horse. There was smearing over with pitch and then setting the body still alive to burn in Nero's garden. There were torments that must not be described, the very pictures of which are enough to make one's eyes weep blood as you look at them. "They were stoned, they were sawn asunder . . . they wandered about in sheepskins and goatskins; being destitute, afflicted, tormented" (Heb. 11:37). These were the roarings of the lion in good Peter's day. Since then, a myriad of martyrs testify how the lion has roared! Let the multitudes who have been put to the most exquisite torture merely because they held to God's Word tell how Satan has roared in days of old! Satan has not half the roar in him now that he had then! Why, he can do nothing at all against us! His roars today are like the hissings of some angry cat. All he can do is use cruel mockings—now and then a wicked slander, a jeer, a caricature, or a witty sentence. What are these? If we cannot bear them, what would we have done when the lion used to really roar? The lion may yet growl again before we leave the face of the earth, for we know not what may happen. But let him roar. We know, blessed be God, that He who is for us is more than all of them who are against us.

There is another kind of furious attack: *the roaring of strong and vehement temptation.* This some of us have felt. Do you know what it is to be caught hold of by a frightful temptation that you hate and yet the clutch of the hand is seconded by an arm so terrific in strength that it drags you right on against your will? You look at the sin, look it in the very face. You feel you cannot do this great wickedness and sin against God, and yet the impulse, strong and stern, mysterious and irresistible, drags you on till you come to the edge of the precipice and look down upon the yawning gulf that threatens to swallow you up. In the last moment, as by the very skin of your teeth, you are delivered, and your foot does not slip; neither do you fall into the hand of the destroyer, yet you have had reason to say, "My steps had almost gone; my feet had well-nigh slipped."

Have you known what it is to have this temptation come again, and again, and again, till you were in a very agony? You felt that you would rather die than thus be perpetually assaulted, for you feared that in an evil hour you might leave your God. This is one of Satan's roarings at you, thrusting his temptation against you like the torments to which they put some of the early martyrs when they laid them down and poured filthy water down their throats in such immense quantities that they were at last killed. So has Satan done with us, pouring down his filth, cramming us with his mire, constraining us as much as possible to yield to temptation. My peculiar temptation has been constant unbelief. I know that God's promise is true and that He that said it will do it, yet does this temptation incessantly assail me: "Doubt Him; distrust Him; He will leave you yet." I can assure you when that temptation is aided by anxiety, it is very hard to stand day by day and say, "No, I cannot doubt my God." That perpetual assaulting, stabbing, and hacking at one's faith is not so easy to endure. O God, deliver us, we pray, and make us more than conquerors by Your Spirit's power!

Satan has another way of roaring. I do not suppose that one in ten of God's people knows anything about this, but Satan can *roar also in the Christian's ear with blasphemies*. I do not allude to those evil thoughts that spring up in the minds of men who in their youth went far into sin. Rather, I allude to those yet more ferocious attacks of Satan when he will inject blasphemous thoughts into the minds of believers who never thought such things before. You know how Bunyan describes it:

> Good Christian had to pass through the valley of the shadow of death. About the midst of this valley, he perceived the mouth of hell to be: and just when he was come over against the mouth of the pit, one of the wicked ones got behind him, and stepped up softly to him, and whisperingly suggested many grievous blasphemies to him, which he verily thought had proceeded from his own mind. This put Christian more to it than anything he had met with before, even to think that now he should blaspheme Him that he so much loved before. Yet, if he could have helped it, he would not have done it. But he had not the discretion either to stop his ears, or to know from whence those blasphemies came.

Seldom do ministers allude to these matters, but inasmuch as such matters trouble some of the people of God, I believe it the duty of a faithful shepherd of the flock to minister to those who are called to pass through this dark and dismal state. Oh, the horrors and terrors that Satan has sometimes caused God's people by the thoughts that were not theirs but proceeded from himself or from some of his fiends! First, Satan suggested the thought so vividly that David cried, "Horror hath taken hold upon me because of the wicked that forsake thy law" (Ps. 119:53). Then, when the thought had flashed for a moment upon the soul, Satan gave a second horror by saying, "You are not a child of God, or you would not have so vile a nature." Whereas you never thought it at all, it was Satan's suggestion, not yours. Then, having laid his sin at your door, Satan has turned accuser of the brethren and sought to cast down your faith from its excellency by making you imagine that you had committed the unpardonable sin. If he roars against you—either with persecution or temptation or diabolical insinuations—take the language of Peter: "Whom resist stedfast in faith, knowing that the same afflictions are accomplished in your brethren that are in the world."

Satan's Ultimate Aim

"Seeking whom he may devour." Nothing less than the perfection and complete salvation of a Christian is the heart's desire of our Savior. The reverse is true of Satan, who can never be content till he sees the believer utterly devoured. Nothing short of the total destruction of a believer will ever satisfy our adversary. Satan would rend the believer in pieces, break his bones, and utterly destroy him if he could. Do not, therefore, indulge the thought that the main purpose of Satan is to make you miserable. Satan is pleased with that, but that is not his ultimate end. Sometimes he may even make you happy, for he has dainty poisons sweet to the taste that he administers to God's people. If he feels that our destruction can be more readily achieved by sweets than by bitters, he certainly would prefer that which would best effect his end. Indeed, it is a stern temptation to be left at ease. When we think we have no occasion for our sword, we begin to unbuckle it from our side; we strip off our armor piece by piece, and then it is that we become most exposed to the attack of our enemies.

Satan will be glad enough, no doubt, to see your faith weakened, but his aim is to destroy that faith so that you may not believe in God to the saving of your soul. Satan will be pleased enough if he can throw mire into the eyes of your hope, but he will never be satisfied till he puts those eyes out altogether and sends you, like Samson, to grind at the mill. Let us take this for our comfort: if it is Satan's desire that we may be utterly destroyed, in that at least he is certain to be defeated. When it comes to the question of who shall win the victory—Christ, the Eternal Son of God, or Satan, the prince of the power of the air—we need have no doubt as to which shall succeed.

The battle is not ours; it is the mighty God's. He that once broke this serpent's head still wages war with him. Not one of those for whom Christ died and on whom He set His love shall ever be given up to the power of His adversary. Count it your joy that Satan may worry but he cannot rend, he may wound but he cannot kill, he may get his foot upon you to make a full end of you but you shall yet start up with fresh strength and say, "Rejoice not against me, O mine enemy: when I fall, I shall arise; when I sit in darkness, the Lord shall be a light unto me" (Mic. 7:8).

How We May Overcome This Adversary

"*Whom resist stedfast in the faith.*" This is our first means of defense. When Satan attacks us as an angel of light, we need not so much resist by open antagonism as by flight. There are some temptations that are to be overcome only by running away from them, but when Satan roars, we must raise the shout and the war cry. To run *then* would be cowardice and must entail certain destruction.

Suppose now that Satan roars with *persecution,* or suppose you are slandered, villified, abused—will you give way? Then are you undone. Will you say, "No, never. By Him who called me to this work, I will see this battle out." You have done well: you have resisted, and you will win the day. Has he assailed you with some temptation obnoxious to your spirit? Yield an inch, and you are undone, but become more watchful and vigilant over yourself in that particular sin, and resistance must certainly bring victory. Or has he injected blasphemy? Resist. Be more prayerful every time he is more active. He will soon give it up if he finds that his attacks drive you to Christ. Often has Satan been nothing but a big black dog to drive Christ's sheep nearer to the Master. Match Satan by turning his temptations to good account, and he will soon give up that method of warfare.

Resist him. But how? "Stedfast in the faith." Seek to obtain a clear knowledge of the doctrines of the gospel, and then get a good grip of them. Be ready to die rather than give up a particle of God's revealed truth. This will make you strong. Then take hold of the promises of God which are yea and amen in Christ Jesus. Know that to every doctrine there is some opposite promise. Have ready for every attack some strong word commencing with "It is written."

All the water outside a ship cannot sink it. It is the water inside that perils the ship's safety. So if your faith can keep its hold and you can say, "Though he slay me yet will I trust in him," Satan may batter your shield, but he has not wounded your flesh. The conflict may be long, but the victory is absolutely sure. Keep near to the cross, and you are safe. Throw your arms around the dying Savior. Let the droppings of His blood fall on your sins, and even if you cannot see Him, still believe in Him. Then let Satan roar, he cannot hurt; let him rage, his fury is vain; he may only show his teeth, for he certainly cannot bite. "Whom resist, stedfast in the faith."

There is another word added for our comfort: "Knowing that the same afflictions are accomplished in your brethren that are in the world." This is well sketched by John Bunyan in the picture I alluded to in the Valley of the Shadow of Death.

> As Christian was going along the exceedingly narrow pathway, with a deep ditch on one side and a dangerous quag upon the other, he came to a stand, and he had half a thought to go back; and then again he thought he might be halfway through the valley; so he resolved to go on. And while he pondered and mused, he heard the voice of a man as going before him, saying, "Yea, though I walk through the valley of the shadow of death, I will fear no evil, for thou art with me." Then he was glad, and that for these reasons. He gathered from thence that some who feared God were in this valley as well as himself; that God was with them, though they perceived him not; that he hoped to have company by-and-bye. So he went on, and called to him that was before, but he knew not what to answer for that he also thought himself to be alone.

Here honest John brings our experience to life. How often have we felt, "I did not think that anybody else ever felt as I feel." This text stands to refute our supposition: "The same afflictions are accomplished in your brethren that are in the world." Certainly your Lord has been there before, for He was tempted in all points like as you are. Scripture says that all your brethren have had some participation in your trials. As they came through the temptation safe and unharmed, so shall you. As they testified that their light afflictions worked out for them a far more exceeding and eternal weight of glory, so that shall be your testimony. As they have overcome and now circle the throne of God clothed in pure white garments, so shall you. You shall come out of every trial and every struggle except that which it is well to lose—your dross and your rust. You shall come forth from the deep waters washed, cleansed, and purified.

Look to His agony and bloody sweat, His cross, His passion, His death, His burial, His resurrection, His ascension, and you shall find a balm for every fear, a cordial for every distress. All that you want and all that your heart can ever desire are most surely to be found in Christ Jesus your Lord.

*T*he history of the Old Testament is a history of Satan endeavoring to hinder the work of the Lord. It has been the same since the days of the Lord Jesus Christ. When Jesus was on earth, Satan hindered Him. Satan dared to attack the Lord to His face; and when that failed, Pharisees, Sadducees, Herodians, and men of all sorts hindered Jesus. When the apostles began their ministry, Herod and the Jews sought to hinder them; and when persecution failed, all sorts of heresies and schisms broke out in the church: Satan still hindered them. In a very short time, the glory had departed from the church and the luster of truth was gone, because by false doctrine, lukewarmness, and worldliness, Satan hindered them. When the Reformation dawned, if God raised up a Luther, the devil brought out an Ignatius Loyola to hinder. Since the first hour struck in which goodness came into conflict with evil, it has never ceased to be true that Satan hindered us. From all points of the compass, all along the line of battle, in the vanguard and in the rear, at the dawn of day and in the midnight, Satan hindered. If we toil in the field, he seeks to break the plow; if we build the walls, he labors to cast down the stones; if we would serve God in suffering or in conflict—everywhere Satan hinders us.

Chapter Eight

Satanic Hindrances

Satan hindered us—1 Thessalonians 2:18.

PAUL, SILAS, AND TIMOTHY seriously de-
sired to visit the church at Thessalonica, but they were unable to
do so for the remarkable reason, "Satan hindered us." *It was not
from a lack of desire*, for they had a deep attachment to the Thessalonians and longed to see them again. They said to the Thessalonians, "We give thanks to God always for you all, making mention
of you in our prayers: Remembering without ceasing your work
of faith, and labour of love, and patience of hope in our Lord Jesus
Christ, in the sight of God and our Father" (1 Thess. 1:2–3). Their
desire was overruled as to visiting the church together, but being
anxious for the church's welfare, they sent Timothy alone to minister for a time in the church's midst. It was not a lack of desire
that hindered them but a lack of power. *And they were not prevented
by God's special providence.* We find on certain occasions that Paul
was not allowed to go precisely where his heart would have led
him: "They were forbidden of the Holy Ghost to preach the word
in Asia" (Acts 16:6). They could not, however, trace their absence
from Thessalonica to any divine intervention; it appeared to them
to proceed from the great adversary: "Satan hindered us."

It would be useless to affirm dogmatically how Satan did this, but we may form a reasonable conjecture. One theory is that Satan hindered Paul by raising such a storm of persecution against him at Berea and other places that it was wise to delay his visit till the storm was past. Yet this could hardly have been the only hindrance, for Paul was so courageous that no fear of opposition would have kept him away. Like a truly valiant champion, Paul delighted to be found in the thick of his foes. Possibly the antagonism of the various philosophers whom he met with at Athens and the heresies at Corinth, from which it seems that this epistle was written, may have called for his presence on the scene of action. Paul felt that he could not leave struggling churches to their enemies; he must contend with the grievous wolves and unmask the evil ones who wore the garb of angels of light.

Satan had moved the enemies of the truth to industrious opposition, and thus the apostle and his companions were hindered from going to Thessalonica. Or it may be that Satan had excited dissensions and discords in the churches that Paul was visiting, and therefore Paul was obliged to stop first in one and then in another to settle their differences—to bring to bear the weight of his own spiritual influence upon the various divided sections of the church to restore them to unity. Whether persecution or philosophic heresy or the divisions of the church were the outward instrument we cannot tell, but Satan was assuredly the prime mover.

You may perhaps wonder why the devil should care so much about Paul and his companions and their whereabouts. Why should the devil be so interested in keeping these three men from that particular church? This question leads us to observe what a wonderful importance is attached to the influence of Christians. Here is the master of all evil, the prince of the power of the air, intently watching the journeying of three humble men, and apparently far more concerned about their movements than about the doings of Nero or Tiberius. These despised heralds of mercy were Satan's most dreaded foes. They preached that name that makes hell tremble. They declared the righteousness against which satanic hate always vents itself with its utmost power. With malicious glance the archenemy watched their daily path, and with cunning hand hindered them at all points. It strikes us that Satan was desirous to keep these apostolic men from the church of Thessalonica because the church was young and weak and Satan thought that he might yet slay the young child. Moreover, Satan has of old a fierce hatred of the preaching of the gospel, and possibly there had been no public declaration of the truth throughout Thessalonica since Paul had gone and he was afraid lest the firebrands of the gospel truth should be again flung in among the masses and a great fire break out. Besides, Satan always hates Christian fellowship; it is his policy to keep Christians apart. Anything that can divide saints from one another he delights in. He attaches far more importance to godly fellowship than we do. Since union is strength, he does his best to promote separation, and so he would keep Paul away that they might miss the strength that always flows from Christian love.

This is not the only occasion on which Satan has hindered good men. Indeed, this has been his practice in all ages, and we have selected this one particular incident that those who are hindered by Satan may draw instruction from it and that no one think it strange when a fiery trial comes upon them.

Satanic Hindrances to the Work of God

Wherever Satan can, he hinders the work of God. "Satan hindered us" is the testimony that all the saints in heaven will bear against the archenemy. This is the witness of all who have written a holy line on the historic page or carved a consecrated name on the rock of immortality.

In sacred writ, we find Satan interfering to hinder the completeness of *the personal character of individual saints*. Job was perfect and upright before God and to all appearance would persevere in producing a finished picture of what the believer in God should be. Indeed he had so lived that the archfiend could find no fault with his actions and only dared to impute wrong motives to him: "Hast not thou made an hedge about him, and about his house, and about all that he hath on every side?" (Job 1:10). Satan sought to turn the life blessing that Job was giving to God into a curse, and therefore he buffeted him sorely. He stripped Job of all his substance. The evil messengers trod upon one another's heels, and their tidings of woe ceased only when his goods were all destroyed and his children had all perished.

The poor afflicted parent was then smitten in his bone and flesh till he was left to sit upon a dunghill and scrape himself with a potsherd. Even then the patient one did not sin. Therefore Satan made another attempt to hinder his retaining his holy character. He excited Job's wife to say, "Dost thou still retain thy integrity? curse God, and die" (Job 2:9). This was a great and grievous hindrance to the completion of Job's marvelous career, but glory to God, the man of patience not only overcame Satan but also made Satan a steppingstone to a yet greater height of illustrious virtue, for you know the patience of Job, and you would not have known it had Satan not illuminated it with the blaze of flaming afflictions. Had the vessel not been burned in the furnace, the bright colors had not been so fixed and abiding.

The trial through which Job passed brought out the luster of Job's matchless endurance in submission and resignation to God. Just as the enemy of old beset the patriarch to hinder his perseverance in the fair path of excellence, so will he do with us. Beware of boasting, for your virtue will yet be tried. Satan will direct his schemes against that very virtue of which you are the most famous. The birds will peck at your ripest fruit, and the wild boar will dash his tusks at your choicest vines. How often have increased godliness, generosity of character, and fidelity of behavior been hindered by satanic malice?

This is not the enemy's only business, for he is very serious in hindering *the freedom of the Lord's redeemed ones*. When the children of Israel were in captivity in Egypt, God's servant stood before their haughty oppressor with his rod in his hand, and in Jehovah's name he declared, "Thus saith the LORD, Let my people go, that they may serve me." A sign was required. The rod was cast upon the ground, and it became a serpent. At this point, Satan hindered. Jannes and Jambres withstood Moses. We read that the magicians did so with their enchantments. Whether by devilish arts or by sleight of hand, they did the devil's service, and they did it well. Pharoah's heart was hardened when he saw that the magicians worked, in appearance, the selfsame miracles that Moses worked. Take this as a type of Satan's hindrances to the Word of the Lord. Christ's servants came forth to preach the gospel; their ministry was attended with signs and wonders. "My kingdom is shaken," said the prince of evil, and immediately he sent magicians to work lying signs and wonders without number.

Apocryphal wonders were and are as plentiful as the frogs of Egypt. No sooner was the gospel preached than Satan had hatched counterfeits of various orders. If you study well the spirit and genious of the great antichrist, you will see that its great power lies in its being an exceedingly clever counterfeit of the gospel of the Lord Jesus Christ. As far as tinsel could counterfeit gold and candlelight could rival the sun in its glory, the antichrist has copied God's great masterpiece, the gospel of our Lord Jesus Christ. To this day, as God's servants scatter the pure gold of truth, their worst enemies are those who utter worthless coin on which they have feloniously stamped the image and superscription of the King of kings.

You have another case further on in history—and all Old Testament history is typical of what is going on around us now. God was about to give a most wonderful system of instruction to Israel in the wilderness and to the human race, by way of type and ceremony. Aaron and his sons were selected to represent the great High Priest of our salvation—the Lord Jesus Christ. In every garment that they wore, there was a symbolical significance. Every vessel of the sanctuary in which they ministered taught a lesson. Every single act of worship, whether the sprinkling of blood or the burning of incense, was made to teach precious and important truths to the sons of men. How God declared Himself and the glory of the coming Messiah in the persons of Aaron and his sons! What then? With this Satan interfered. Moses and Aaron could say, "Satan hindered us." Korah, Dathan, and Abiram arrogantly claimed a right to the priesthood, and on a certain day they stood forth with brazen censers in their hands, thrusting themselves impertinently into the office. The earth opened and swallowed them up alive: true prophecy of what shall become of those who thrust themselves into the office of the priesthood where none but Jesus Christ can stand.

You may see the parallel today. The doctrine of a finished atonement and completed sacrifice of Christ seemed likely to overrun the world. It was such a gracious unfolding of the divine mind that Satan could not look upon it without desiring to hinder it.

Therefore, look and you find churches where men to this very day arrogate to themselves a priesthood other than that which is common to all the saints. Some even claim to offer a daily sacrifice, to celebrate an unbloody sacrifice at the thing that they call an altar; and they claim to have power to forgive sin, saying to sick and dying people, "By authority committed unto me, I absolve thee from all thy sins." This is the great hindrance to the spread of the gospel. Thus are we made to cry, "Satan hindereth us."

Take another instance of satanic hatred. When Joshua had led the tribes across the Jordan, the people were to attack the various cities that God had given them for a heritage, and from Dan to Beersheba the whole land was to be theirs. After the taking of Jericho, the first contact into which they came with the heathen Canaanites ended in a disastrous defeat to the servants of God. "They fled," it is written, "before the men of Ai" (Josh. 7:4). Here again you hear the cry, "Satan hindered us." Achan had taken the accursed thing and hidden it in his tent; therefore, no victory could be won by Israel till his sacrilege had been put away. This is symbolic of today's church. We might go from victory to victory, both in our home and in foreign missions, if it were not that we have Achans in the camp. Hypocrisy within the church—those who make a profession of faith as the means of getting wealth, those who covet the goodly Babylonish garment and the wedge of gold, are those who cut the sinews of Zion's strength and prevent the Israel of God from going forth to victory. Little do we know how Satan has hindered us. How many more might have been added to the church had it not been for the coldness of some, the indifference of others, the inconsistency of a few, and the worldliness of many more! Satan hinders us not merely by direct opposition but also by sending Achans into the midst of our camp.

Here is one more picture. View the building of Jerusalem after it had been destroyed by the Babylonians. When Ezra and Nehemiah were found to build, the devil was sure to stir up Sanballat and Tobiah to cast down. There was never a revival of godliness without a revival of the old enmity. If ever the church of God is to be built, it will be in troublesome times. When God's servants are active, Satan is not without vigilant soldiers who seek to counteract their efforts.

The history of the Old Testament is a history of Satan endeavoring to hinder the work of the Lord. It has been the same since the days of the Lord Jesus Christ. When Jesus was on earth, Satan hindered Him. Satan dared to attack the Lord to His face; and when that failed, Pharisees, Sadducees, Herodians, and men of all sorts hindered Jesus. When the apostles began their ministry, Herod and the Jews sought to hinder them; and when persecution failed, all sorts of heresies and schisms broke out in the church: Satan still hindered them. In a very short time, the glory had departed from the church and the luster of truth was gone, because by false doctrine, lukewarmness, and worldliness, Satan hindered them. When the Reformation dawned, if God raised up a Luther, the devil brought out an Ignatius Loyola to hinder. Here in England, if God had His Latimers and Wycliffes, the devil had his Gardiners and Bonners. When Whitefield and Wesley thundered like the voice of God, there were reprobates found to hinder them, to hold them up to shame. Since the first hour struck in which goodness came into conflict with evil, it has never ceased to be true that Satan hindered us. From all points of the compass, all along the line of battle, in the vanguard and in the rear, at the dawn of day and in the midnight, Satan hindered. If we toil in the field, he seeks to break the plow; if we build the walls, he labors to cast down the stones; if we would serve God in suffering or in conflict— everywhere Satan hinders us.

The Many Ways Satan Hinders

The prince of evil is very busy in hindering *those who are just coming to Jesus Christ.* Here he spends the main part of his skill. Some of us who know the Savior recall the fierce conflicts we had with Satan when we first looked to the cross and lived. Once you give attention to the eternal things, you become the target of deep distress of mind. Do not marvel at this. This is usual—so usual as to be almost universal. It is possible that your sins are brought to your remembrance, and now it is hinted to you by satanic malice that they are too great to be pardoned, to which you should tell Satan this truth: "All manner of sin and blasphemy shall be forgiven unto men" (Matt. 12:31).

It is possible that the sin against the Holy Ghost molests you.

You read that whosoever shall speak a word against the Holy Ghost shall never be forgiven, and you wonder if you have committed this sin. One fact may cheer you: if you repent of your sins, you have not committed the unpardonable offense, since that sin necessitates hardness of heart forever; and so long as a man has any tenderness of conscience and any softness of spirit, he has not so renounced the Holy Spirit as to have lost His presence.

It may be that you are the victim of blasphemous thoughts. Torrents of the filth of hell may have poured through your soul. Do not be astonished at this, for it is possible for those who delight in holiness and are pure in heart to be sorely tried with thoughts that were never born in hearts but were injected into them—suggestions born in hell—not in their spirits, to be hated and loathed, but cast into their minds that they might hinder. Though Satan may hinder you, yet dare to trust in Jesus; I warrant you, there shall be a joy and peace in believing that shall overcome him of whom we read that he has "hindered us."

Satan is sure to hinder Christians *when they are sincerely in prayer*. Have you not frequently found when you have been most earnest in prayer that something or other will start across your mind to make you cease? I mean that just when prayer would be the most successful, we are tempted to stop. If the temptation did not come in that shape, yet it would come in another—to cease to pray because prayer after all could not avail.

The same is true of *Christians when under the promptings of the Spirit of God or when planning any good work.* You have been prompted sometimes to speak to someone, but you have not done it—Satan hindered you. You have felt you should visit a certain person and help him but have not done it—Satan hindered you. You know a missionary working in some district destitute of truth, and you have thought, "I have a little money that I might give to help," but then it has come to you that there is another way of spending the money more profitably on your family—so Satan has hindered you. If he possibly can, Satan will come upon God's people when they are pursuing a new Christian work that he may murder their infant plans and cast these suggestions of the Holy Spirit out of their minds.

How often, too, has Satan hindered us *when we have entered into the work.* In fact, we never should expect a success unless we hear the devil making a noise. I have taken it as a certain sign that I am doing little good when the devil is quiet. It is generally a sign that Christ's kingdom is coming when men begin to lie against you and slander you. Oh, those blessed tempests! Do not give me calm weather when the air is still and heavy and when lethargy is creeping over one's spirit. Lord, send a hurricane, give us a little stormy weather. When the lightning flashes and the thunder rolls, God's servants know that the Lord is abroad and that His right hand is no longer in His bosom, that the moral atmosphere will get clear, that God's kingdom will come and His will be done on earth, even as it is in heaven.

"Peace, peace, peace" is the flap of the dragon's wings; the stern voice that proclaims perpetual war is the voice of the Captain of our salvation. Expect fightings, and you will not be disappointed. Whitefield used to say that some divines would go from the first of January to the end of December with a perfectly whole skin— the devil never thought them worth attacking. But, said he, let us begin to preach the gospel of Jesus Christ with all our might and soul and strength, and men will soon put a fool's cap on our heads and begin laughing at us and ridiculing us: but if so, so much the better. We are not alarmed, because Satan hinders us.

Nor will he hinder us only in working: he will hinder us also *in seeking to unite with one another*. As local churches, we are about to make an effort to come closer together, but I should not wonder but what Satan will hinder us. Only through prayer will Satan be put to rout and the union of churches be accomplished. And within a church, I should not marvel if Satan should try to thrust in the cloven foot to hinder our walking in love and peace and unity.

Detecting Satanic Hindrances

We are not always to conclude when we are hindered and disappointed in our intentions that Satan has done it, for it may very often be the good providence of God. But how can I tell when Satan hinders me? First, *by the object*: to prevent our glorifying God. If anything has happened to you that has prevented your growing holy, effective, humble, and sanctified, you may trace that to Satan. If the distinct object of the interference has been that you may be turned from righteousness to sin, from the object you may guess the author. It is not God who does this, but Satan. Yet you should know that God does sometimes put apparent hindrances in the way of His people, even in reference to their usefulness and growth in grace, but then His object is still to be considered. It is to try His saints and so to strengthen them, while the object of Satan is to turn people away from the right road and make them take the crooked way.

You can tell the suggestions of Satan by *the method* in which they come: God employs good motives, Satan bad ones. If that which has turned you away from your object has been a bad thought, a bad doctrine, a bad teaching, a bad motive—it never came from God; it must be from Satan.

You can also tell the suggestions of Satan from *their nature*. Whenever a hindrance to effectiveness is pleasing, gratifying to you, consider that it came from Satan. Satan never brushes the feathers of his birds the wrong way; he generally deals with us according to our tastes and likings. He flavors his bait to his fish. He knows exactly how to deal with each man and to put that motive that accords with the suggestions of our carnality. If the difficulty in your way is rather contrary to yourself than for yourself, it comes from God, but if that which now is a hindrance brings you gain or pleasure in any way, rest assured it came from Satan.

We can tell the suggestions of Satan by their season. Hindrances to prayer, for instance, if they are satanic, come *out of the natural course and relation of human thoughts*. It is a law of mental science that one thought suggests another, and the next the next, and so on, as the link of a chain draws on another. But satanic temptations do not come in the regular order of thinking—they dash upon the mind out of nowhere. When my soul is in prayer, it would be unnatural that I should then blaspheme, yet the blasphemy comes. It is therefore clearly satanic and not from my own mind. If I am set upon doing my Master's will and presently a wretched thought assails me, the thought may be at once ejected as not being mine and set down to the account of the devil. By these means I think we can tell when Satan hinders, when it is our own heart, or when it is of God. We should carefully watch that we do not put the saddle on the wrong horse. Do not blame the devil when it is yourself; on the other hand, when the Lord puts a bar in your way, do not say, "That is Satan," and so go against the providence of God. It may be difficult at times to see the way of duty, but if you go to the throne of God in prayer, you will soon discover it.

Dealing with Satanic Hindrances

I have but one piece of advice, and that is, *go on*—hindrance or no hindrance—in the path of duty as God the Holy Ghost enables you. If Satan hinders you, I have already said that this *opposition should cheer you*. If you can trace the opposition distinctly to Satan, do not sit down and fret. It is a great thing that you can actually trouble the great prince of darkness and win his hate. It makes the race of man the more noble that it comes in conflict with a race of spirits and stands foot to foot even with the prince of darkness himself. Stand out against him because *you have an opportunity of making a greater gain than you could have had had he been quiet*. You could never have had a victory over him had you not engaged in conflict with him. If devils did not oppose my path from earth to heaven, I might travel joyously, peacefully, safely, but certainly without renown. But now, when every step is contested in winning our pathway to glory, every single step is covered with immortal fame. Press on then; the more opposition, the more honor.

Be vigilant against these hindrances when you consider *what you lose if you do not resist him and overcome*. To allow Satan to overcome me would be eternal ruin to my soul. Certainly it would forever blast all hopes of my usefulness. If I retreat and turn my back in the day of battle, what will the rest of God's servants say? What shouts of derision will ring over the battlefield? How will the banner of the covenant be trailed in the mire? We must not— we dare not—play the coward. We dare not give way to insinuations of Satan and turn from the Master, for the defeat were then too dreadful to be endured. Let me feed your courage with the recollection that *your Lord and Master has overcome*. See Him there before you. He has fought the enemy and broken his head. Satan has been completely worsted by the Captain of your salvation, and that victory was representative—He fought and won it for you. You have to contend with a defeated foe who knows and feels his disgrace; and though he may fight with desperation, yet he fights not with true courage, for he is hopeless of ultimate victory. Strike, then, for Christ has smitten him. Down with him, for Jesus has had him under His foot. Triumph is yours, for the Captain has triumphed before you.

Lastly, remember that *you have a promise* to strengthen you. "Resist the devil, and he will flee from you" (James 4:7). Christian minister, do not think of sending in your resignation because the church is divided and the enemy is making headway. Resist the devil. Flee not, but make *him* flee. Christian young people, though Satan hinders you very much, redouble your resolve. It is because he is afraid of you that Satan resists you, because he would rob you of the great blessing that is now descending on your head. Resist him and stand fast. You who plead in prayer, do not let go of your hold upon the Covenant Angel, for now that Satan hinders you, it is because the blessing is descending. You who are seeking Christ, close not those eyes, turn not away your face from Calvary's streaming tree. Now that Satan hinders you, it is because the night is almost over and the daystar begins to shine. You who are most sorrowfully tried, most borne down, yours is the brighter hope. Be now courageous, play the man for God, for Christ, for your own soul; and yet the day shall come when you with your Master shall ride triumphant through the streets of the New Jerusalem—sin, death and hell captive at your chariot wheels, and you with your Lord crowned as victor, having overcome through the blood of the Lamb.

Soldiers, look to your heads. A wound in the head is a serious matter. Since the head is a vital part, we need to well protect it. The heart needs to be guarded with the breastplate, but the head needs just as much protection, for even if a man is true-hearted, if a shot should go through his brain, his body ends strewn on the plain. There are Christians who get their hearts warmed and think that is enough. Give me above everything else a good warm heart, but, oh, to have that warm heart coupled with a head that is well taken care of. Do you know that a hot head and a hot heart together do a great deal of mischief, but with a hot heart and a cool head, you may do a world of service for the Master. Have right doctrine in the head, and then set the soul on fire, and you will soon win the world. There is no standing in the person's way whose head and heart are both right, but many Christians have caused serious trouble by neglecting the head. They have been almost useless because they have not taken care of their brains. They arrive in heaven, but they have few victories because they have never been able to clearly understand the doctrine—they have not been able to give a reason for the hope that lies within them. They have not, in fact, looked well to the helmet that was to cover their heads.

Chapter Nine

The Christian's Helmet

And for an helmet, the hope of salvation—1 Thessalonians 5:8.

THE VERY MENTION OF A HELMET serves to remind every believer that he is a soldier. If you were not soldiers, you would not need armor, but being soldiers, you need to be clad in armor from head to foot. The Christian soldier has been enlisted under the banner of the cross to fight against the powers of darkness until he wins the victory. But we all need to be reminded that soldiering in a time of war is never a pleasant occupation, and the flesh constantly attempts to give it over. "For here we have no continuing city" (Heb. 13:14) is a truth that we know, yet most of us try to make the earth as comfortable for ourselves as if it were to be our abiding residence. Too many believers act as if they could be the friends of the world and the friends of God at the same time. Settle the matter once for all that you are a soldier.

Did you dream that when you came to faith in Christ, the conflict would be over? Ah, it was only the beginning. Like Caesar, you crossed the Rubicon and declared war against your deadly enemy. You drew your sword, and you did not sheath it. Your proper note on joining the church is not one of congratulations that the victory is won but one of preparation, for now the trumpet sounds and the fight begins. You are a soldier at all times. Whether you sit at your table or go out into the world, you are a soldier. Never take off your armor, for if you do, in some unguarded moment, you may meet with serious wounds. But *keep your armor always about you and be watchful,* for you are always in the midst of enemies wherever you are. Even when surrounded by friends, there are still unseen evil spirits who watch for your halting. You must not put up your sword, for you are to wrestle in high places against principalities and powers and spiritual wickednesses against which you must ever be on watch.

Nor are you a soldier in barracks or at home, but *you are a soldier in an enemy's country.* Your place is either in the trenches patiently waiting for the battle to begin or in the thick of battle. More or less, according to your circumstances, you are exposed to the foe, and that at every period of life.

You are *in the country of a malicious enemy.* If you fall, it is death. The world never forgives a Christian. It hates him with a perfect hatred, and it longs to do him harm. Let the world see you commit even half a fall, and it will soon report and magnify it. What might be done by others without notice, if it were done by a believer would be reported and misrepresented. The world understands that you are its natural antagonist. Satan perceives in you a representative of his old enemy, the Lord Jesus, and you may rest assured that he will take advantage of every opportunity to destroy you.

You have to fight with one, too, *who never yet made a truce. You* may come to terms and parley, but the powers of evil never do. *You* may hang out the white flag if you like. The foe may seem for a time as though he gave you credit, but do you never give your foe any credit? He hates you when he seems to love you best. "Dread the Greeks, even when they bring gifts," said the tradition of old, and let the Christian dread the world most when it puts on its softest speeches. Stand on guard, you warriors of the cross, when least you fear. The cringing foe will come behind you and stab you under the pretense of friendship. Your Master was betrayed by a kiss, and so will you be unless you watch in prayer.

You face an enemy *who never can make peace with you, nor can you ever make peace with him.* If you become at peace with sin, sin has conquered you, and it is impossible, unless you give up the fight and yield your neck to everlasting thraldom, that you should ever be at peace for as much as a moment. Oh, Christian, see how guarded you should be! How needful to be clothed with your armor! How needful to have it of the right kind, to keep it bright, and to wear it constantly! Heaven is the land where your sword should be sheathed; there shall you hang the banner high, but here we wrestle with the foe and must do so till we cross the torrent of death. Right up to the river's edge must the conflict be waged. Foot by foot and inch by inch must all the land to Canaan's happy shore be won. Not a step can be taken without conflict and strife. But once there, you may lay aside your helmet and put on your crown, put away your sword and take your palm branch. Your fingers shall no longer need to learn war, but your hearts shall learn the music of the happy songsters of the skies. This, then, is the first thought: you are a soldier.

Protection for Your Head

Soldiers, look to your heads. A wound in the head is a serious matter. Since the head is a vital part, we need to well protect it. The heart needs to be guarded with the breastplate, but the head needs just as much protection, for even if a man is true-hearted, if a shot should go through his brain, his body ends strewn on the plain. There are Christians who get their hearts warmed and think that is enough. Give me above everything else a good warm heart, but, oh, to have that warm heart coupled with a head that is well taken care of. Do you know that a hot head and a hot heart together do a great deal of mischief, but with a hot heart and a cool head, you may do a world of service for the Master. Have right doctrine in the head, and then set the soul on fire, and you will soon win the world. There is no standing in the person's way whose head and heart are both right, but many Christians have caused serious trouble by neglecting the head. They have been almost useless because they have not taken care of their brains. They arrive in heaven, but they have few victories because they have never been able to clearly understand the doctrine—they have not been able to give a reason for the hope that lies within them. They have not, in fact, looked well to the helmet that was to cover their heads.

The text refers us to our head because it speaks of a helmet, and a helmet is useful only to the head. Among other reasons that we should preserve the head in the day of battle, let us give these. *The head is peculiarly liable to the temptations of Satan, of self, and of fame.* It is difficult to stand on a high temple pinnacle as Christ did in His temptation without the brain beginning to reel. And if God takes a man and puts him on a high pinnacle of usefulness, the man needs to protect his head. If a person has considerable wealth, there is a great danger in that wealth unless there is a wealth of grace as well. If a man has a good reputation, his sphere may not be very large, but if everybody praises him, he also will need to have his head well protected, for the little praise, even though it might come from fools, would be too much for a fool. The fining-pot for silver, and praise for the man.

A man who can stand commendation can stand anything. Probably the severest trial that a Christian has to bear is the trial that comes from his kind but inconsiderate friends who would puff him up if they could by telling him what a fine fellow he is. If your friends will not do this, you probably have a friend within named *self* who will; and if *you* should forget to praise yourself, the devil will not, and hence the need of having a helmet so that when you are successful, when you are getting on in life, when friends are speaking well of you, you may not get intoxicated with praise. Oh, to have a good, cool helmet to put on your brain when it begins to get a little hot with praise, so that you may still stand fast and not be borne down by vanity. O Vanity, Vanity, Vanity, how many have you slain! How many who stood on the very brink of greatness have stumbled on this rock! People who seemed as though they would enter heaven, but that a little of honor, some glittering bribe, or a golden opportunity has turned them aside, and they fell. Take care of your heads.

And is not *the head liable to attacks from skepticism*? Doubts assail from every possible angle, and bullets of skepticism are aimed straight at our brain. What then? As we cannot take Christians out of the way of bullets, we should give them a helmet to preserve them. He who has a hope of salvation—a good hope that he shall see the face of Christ with joy at last—is not afraid of all the quibbles of skepticism. He may hear them all and for a moment be staggered by them as a soldier might be who had a sudden shock or even a wound, but after a while, he recovers himself and feels sound enough to enter into the conflict again. When a man gets a stake in Christianity, he gets to be very, very conservative of the old-fashioned truth. He cannot give up the Bible then, because it is a broad land of wealth to him. He cannot give up Christ, for He is *his* Savior. He cannot give up a single promise, because that promise is so dear to his own soul. The helmet of salvation, then, will preserve the head in times of skepticism.

The head is very greatly in danger *from the attacks of personal unbelief.* Who among us has not doubted his own interest in Christ? Happy are you who are free from such trouble. But there are seasons with some of us when we turn our title deeds over and are sometimes afraid they might not be genuine. There are times when, if we could, we would give the world to know that we are Christ's. This is very dangerous to our heads. But the man who has the helmet of a right, sound, God-given hope of salvation from the Holy Spirit, when these doubts and fears come, they may distress him for a little while, but he knows the smell of gunpowder and is not afraid. In the midst of all Satan's accusations, or the uprisings of his old corruptions, or the threatenings of the flesh and of the world, this man stands calm and unmoved because he wears as a helmet the hope of salvation.

Nor are these all the danger to which the head is exposed. *Some believers are attacked by threatenings from the world,* which brings down its double-handled sword with a tremendous blow upon the heads of many Christians. "You will suffer the loss of all things for Christ if you are such a fanatic. You will be poor, your children will starve, your wife will be worse than a widow, if you are such a fool." "Ah," says the Christian, "I can afford to be poor; I can afford to be despised; but I have a hope of salvation." And the blow, when it comes, does not go through his head but falls on the helmet, and the world's sword gets blunted. So by the use of this blessed helmet he is not destroyed by the threatenings of the world.

We want our young people to wear this helmet, too, *because of the errors of the times.* Young people are tempted on the one side, then the other. This and that you will have cried up. "Lo here" and "Lo there," and there will be many misled who are not the people of God. But the elect are not deceived, because their heads are not vulnerable to these errors, for they wear the hope of salvation, and they are not afraid of all the "ites" and "isms" of the world. Once you get to know Christ personally, the world will count you stupid and obstinate, but you will stand firm and be able to resist all the world's sarcasm and ridicule. He who has made a refuge of Jesus Christ may stand safe, whatever errors may invade the land.

The truth is that the church of God can never be in danger. Every man in whom is the life of God would be as ready to die tomorrow for the truth as our forefathers were in days of persecution. Rest assured there would be found men to stand at the burning stake still if the times required it, and our prisons would not long be without heavenly-minded tenants if the truth needed to be defended by suffering, even unto death. There is always great danger in error. But there is no danger to the man who has his helmet on. No, let the arrows fly thick as hail, and let the foes have all political power and all the prestige of antiquity that they may. A little group of true-hearted Christians will still stand out at the thick of the onslaught and cut their way to glory and victory through whole hosts because their heads are guarded with the heavenly helmet of the hope of salvation. Soldiers, then, take care of your heads.

The Helmet Itself

"The hope of salvation!" This helmet is made up of actual hope that being already saved in Christ Jesus, you should abide unto eternal life. It is a personal hope founded upon personal conviction and is wrought in us by the Holy Spirit.

To begin, then, let me describe this helmet. *Who is its giver?* You ask the soldier where he gets his armor, and he answers from the government stores. That is where we must get our helmets. If you construct a helmet of hope for yourself, it will be of no use to you in the day of battle. The true helmet of hope must come from the heavenly arsenal. You must go to the Divine storehouse, for to God belongs salvation, and the hope of salvation must be given to you by His free grace. A hope of salvation is not purchasable. Our great King does not sell His armor but gives it freely to all who enlist. From head to foot the soldiers of the cross are arrayed by grace.

Do you ask, *who is the maker of this helmet?* Weapons are often valued according to the maker. A known maker gets his own price for his articles. Armorers of old took much trouble with the ancient helmets because a man's life might depend upon that very useful means of defense. So we have here the name of God the Holy Ghost upon this helmet. A hope of salvation is the work of the Holy Spirit in your soul. It is the Spirit who brings us to Jesus, shows us our need of Him, and gives us faith in Him. It is the same Spirit who enables us to hope that we shall endure to the end and enter into eternal life. We have a hope that is supernatural.

Would you inquire further, *of what metal is this helmet made?* We are told that it is made of hope, but it is of the utmost consequence that it be *good* hope. Beware of getting a base hope, a helmet made of cheap metal. There were some helmets that looked very good but were of no more use than brown paper hats; and when a soldier got into the fight with one of them on, the sword went through his skull. Get a good helmet, one made of the right metal. This is what a Christian's hope is made of: the Christian believes that Christ came into the world to save sinners, he trusts Christ to save him, and he hopes that when Christ comes he shall reign with Him— that when the trumpet sounds he shall rise with Christ—and that in heaven he shall have a secure dwelling place at the right hand of the Father.

Some people have a hope, but they do not know where they received it from, nor do they know a reason for it. Hope must have its reason; it must have its weight. Such is the Christian's hope. God has promised to save those who believe. The Christian's hope is not a fancy, not a silly desire. It did not spring up in the night like Jonah's gourd, and it will not wither in a night. The Christian's hope is something that will withstand the crack from a club or a cut from a sharp sword. It is made of good metal. John Bunyan said of a certain sword that it was "a true Jerusalem blade," and I may call this a true Jerusalem helmet, and he who wears it need not fear.

Having shown the metal of which the helmet is made, let me now describe *the strength of the helmet*. The helmet is so strong that under all sorts of assaults, he who wears it is invulnerable. The wearer may stagger under a blow, but he cannot be hurt by it. Recollect what David said. All the troubles in the world attacked David at once and began to beat upon him, giving him many terrible blows. His enemies thought they had certainly ruined him, and David was bleeding and full of wounds. David himself half thought he should die, and he tells us that he would have fainted except that he had a bottle of cordial with him called faith. He says, "I had fainted, unless I had not believed" (Ps. 27:13). But just at the time when the false witnesses thought he would faint and die, suddenly the old hero who slew Goliath made all his enemies fly before him as he cried, "Why art thou cast down, O my soul? and why art thou disquieted within me? hope thou in God" (Ps. 42:5). And he laid about him right and left, as he should: "for I shall yet praise him, who is the health of my countenance, and my God" (Ps. 42:11).

"Hope thou in God," Christian. Oh, that blessed word *HOPE!* New Zealanders call hope "the swimming thought," because it always swims. You cannot drown it; it always keeps its head above the wave. When you think you have drowned the Christian's hope, up it comes and cries again, "Hope thou in God, for I shall yet praise Him!" Hope is the nightingale that sings in the night; faith is the lark that mounts up toward heaven; but hope is the nightingale that cheers the valley of darkness. O Christian, be thankful that you have so strong a helmet as this, which can bear all assaults and keep you unwounded in the midst of the fray!

This hope of salvation *is a helmet that will not come off.* It is of great importance to have a helmet that will not be knocked off the first thing in the fight. The Christian wears a helmet that he cannot get off. There was once a good soldier of Jesus Christ, a good woman who was attacked by a skeptic. When she was very much confounded with some of his knotty questions, she turned around and said to him, "I cannot answer you, sir, but neither can you answer me, for I have something within me that you cannot understand, which makes me feel that I could not give up what I know of Christ for all the world." You see, he could not get her helmet off, and the devil himself cannot drag the Christian's helmet off once it is buckled on. The world can neither give nor take away the hope of a Christian. Such hope comes from God, and He will never withdraw it, for His gifts and calling are without repentance. Once this helmet is put on, we shall hope on and hope ever until we shall see His face at the last.

I should like to inspect your helmet as the commanding officers of old did. The officers, when they went round the regiment, looked not only to see that the men had their helmets but also to see that they had oiled them, for in those times they used to oil their helmets to make them shine and to keep the various joints and buckles in good order. No rust was ever allowed on the helmets, and it is said that when the soldiers marched out with their brazen helmets and their white plumes, they shone most brilliantly in the sun.

David speaks of "anointing the shield." He was speaking of a brazen shield that had to be anointed with oil. When God anoints His people's hope, when He gives His people the oil of joy, their hope begins to shine bright in the light of the Savior's countenance. What a fine array of soldiers they are then! Satan trembles at the gleaming of God's people's swords; he cannot endure to look upon the saints' helmets. But some Christians fail to keep their hope clear; they do not keep it bright. Their hope gets rusty from disuse, and before long it gets to sit uncomfortably on their head, and they get weary with the fight. O Holy Spirit, anoint our heads with fresh oil and let Your saints go forth terrible as an army with banners.

Let it not be overlooked that *the helmet was generally considered to be a place of honor.* The man put his plume in his helmet, he wore his crest frequently there, and in the thick of the fight the captain's plume was seen in the midst of the smoke and dust of battle, and the men pressed to the place where they saw it. The Christian's hope is his honor and glory. I must be unashamed of my hope. I must wear it for beauty and for dignity, and he who has a good hope will be a leader to others. Others will see it and fight with renewed courage, and where he hews a lane of the foes, they will follow him, even as he follows his Lord and Master, who has overcome and sits down upon His Father's throne.

Any Other Helmet

The Lord Jesus provides armor only to those in His service. But Satan gives helmets, too. His helmets are very potent ones. Though the sword of the Spirit can go right through them, nothing else can. Satan can give a headpiece that covers your entire skull—a thick headpiece of indifference, so that no matter what is preached, you do not care.

Then Satan puts a piece in the front of the helmet called a *brazen forehead and a brow of brass*. "What do I care?" is your cry. Next Satan takes care to fit the helmet over your eyes so that you cannot see; though hell itself parade before you, you do not see it. "What do I care?" Satan also knows how to fit the helmet so that it acts as a gag to your mouth so that you never pray. You can swear through it, but you cannot pray. Still you keep to your old cry, "What do I care?"

It is not likely that any sword will get at your head! Arguments will not move you, for the question "What do I care?" is one that cannot very well be argued. I pray God the Holy Spirit to get at your head, notwithstanding that horrible helmet, for if not, God has a way of dealing with such. When you come to die, you will sing another song! When you come to that grim day when eternity is in view, you will not be able to say quite so gaily as you do now, "What do I care?" And when the trumpet rings through earth and heaven, and your body starts up from your grave, and you see the great Judge upon His throne, you will not be saying, "What do I care?" Your head will then be bare to the pitiless tempest of divine wrath. Bareheaded you must be exposed to the everlasting storm that shall descend upon you. And cares will come upon you like a wild deluge when you are banished from His presence and all hope is gone!

Oh, I desire that you take off that other helmet! May God grant you grace to unbuckle it and never put it on again! Do care. It is only a fool who says, "What do I care?" *Surely you care about your soul; surely hell is worth escaping; surely heaven is worth winning; surely that cross on which our Savior died is worth considering; surely that poor soul of yours is worth caring about!* May Jesus Christ bring you to trust Him, and then, unbuckling all that evil armor, you will bow before His cross and kiss His hands, and He will put upon you the golden helmet of a hope of salvation, and you will rise—one of the King's own soldiers—to fight His battles and win an immortal wreath of everlasting victory!

*W*e are glad to find that the shoes are made of excellent material, and what better material can there be than the gospel of peace and the peace that grows out of the gospel? This is what is meant. We believe in a gospel that was formed in the purpose of God from all eternity, designed with infinite wisdom, wrought out at an enormous expense, costing nothing less than the blood of Jesus, brought home by the infinite power of the Holy Spirit; a gospel full of blessings, any one of which would outweigh a world in price; a gospel as free as it is full; a gospel everlasting and immutable; a gospel of which we can never think too much, whose praises we can never exaggerate! It is from this choice gospel that its choicest essence is taken—namely, its peace—and from this peace those sandals are prepared with which a man may tread on the lion and the adder, and even on the fierce burning coals of malice, slander, and persecution. What better shoes can our souls require?

Chapter Ten

Shoes for Pilgrims and Warriors

And your feet shod with the preparation of the gospel of peace—
Ephesians 6:15.

THE CHRISTIAN WAS EVIDENTLY INTENDED
to be in motion, for here are shoes for his feet. His head is provided
with a helmet, for he is to be thoughtful. His heart is covered with
a breastplate, for he is to be a man of feeling. His whole nature is
protected by a shield, for he is called to endurance and caution.
But that he is to be active is certain, for a sword is provided for his
hand and sandals for his feet. To think that a Christian is to be
motionless as a post and inanimate as a stone, or merely pensive
as a weeping willow and passive as a reed shaken by the wind, is
altogether a mistake. God works in us, and His grace is the great
motivating power that secures our salvation. But He does not drug
us into unconscious submission or engineer us into mechanical
motion. Rather, He arouses all our activities by working in us "to
will and to do of his good pleasure." Grace imparts healthy life,
and life rejoices in activity. The Lord never intended His people to
be automatons worked by clockwork or statues cold and dead. He
meant them to have life, to have it abundantly, and in the power
of that life to be full of energy. It is true He makes us lie down in
green pastures, but equally certain is it that He leads us onward

beside still waters. A true believer is an active person; he has feet, and he uses them.

He who marches meets with rough terrain, or if as a warrior he dashes into the thick of conflict, he is assailed with weapons, and therefore he needs footwear suitable to meet his perils. The active and energetic Christian meets with temptations that others do not meet. Idle persons can hardly be said to be in danger; they are a stage beyond that and are already overcome. Satan barely needs to tempt them; they rather tempt him and are a fermenting mass in which sin multiplies exceedingly. But earnest, laborious believers are sure to be assailed, even as fruit-bearing trees are certain to be visited by birds. Satan cannot tolerate a person who serves God earnestly; such a person does damage to the archenemy's dominions and therefore must be incessantly assailed. The prince of darkness will try, if he can, to injure the person's character, to break his communion with God, to spoil the simplicity of his faith, to make him proud of what he is doing, or to make him despair of success. In one way or another he will, if possible, bruise the worker's heel or trip him up or lame him altogether. Because of all these dangers, infinite mercy has provided gospel shoes for the believer's feet, shoes of the best kind, such as only those warriors wear who serve the Lord of Hosts.

The Shoes

The shoes *come from a blessed Maker*, for the believer's feet are to be shod with a divine *preparation*. Many preparations and inventions are used for protecting feet, but this is a preparation in which infinite skill has been displayed and the same wisdom put forth as in the gospel, which is the masterpiece of God. Every portion of the gospel is from God, and all the influence that makes it a gospel of peace is His, and we are therefore thankful to find that we are to wear "the preparation of the gospel of peace." It would not be fitting that he who is helmeted with divine salvation should have shoes of mere human production. Having begun in the Spirit, it would be strange to be made perfect in the flesh. We rejoice that all the pieces of armor that compose our panoply come from the celestial Armorer, whose productions are without flaw.

We are glad to find that *the shoes are made of excellent material,* and what better material can there be than the gospel of peace and the peace that grows out of the gospel? This is what is meant. We believe in a gospel that was formed in the purpose of God from all eternity, designed with infinite wisdom, wrought out at an enormous expense, costing nothing less than the blood of Jesus, brought home by the infinite power of the Holy Spirit; a gospel full of blessings, any one of which would outweigh a world in price; a gospel as free as it is full; a gospel everlasting and immutable; a gospel of which we can never think too much, whose praises we can never exaggerate! It is from this choice gospel that its choicest essence is taken—namely, its peace—and from this peace those sandals are prepared with which a man may tread on the lion and the adder, and even on the fierce burning coals of malice, slander, and persecution. What better shoes can our souls require?

What matchless material for the pilgrim's foot is the peace of the gospel, the preparation of heart and life, which springs of a full knowledge, reception, and experience of the gospel in our souls! It means, first, that *a sense of perfect peace with God* is the grandest thing in all the world with which to travel through life. Let a man know that his sins are forgiven for Christ's sake, that he is reconciled to God by the death of His Son, and that between him and God there is no ground of difference, and what a joyful pilgrim he becomes! When we know that as the Lord looks on us, His glance is full of infinite, undivided affection, that He sees us in Jesus Christ as cleansed from every speck of sin and "accepted in the beloved" (Eph. 1:6), that by virtue of a complete atonement we are forever reconciled to God, then do we march through life without fear, booted and buskined for all the difficulties of the way, ready to plunge without fear through fire and water, thorn and thistle. A man at peace with God dreads neither the ills of life nor the terrors of death; poverty, sickness, persecution, and pain have lost their sting when sin is pardoned. What is there that a man needs to fear when he knows that everything comes from the Father's hand and works his everlasting good?

Goliath had greaves of brass upon his legs, but he is better armed who wears a full assurance of peace with God through the gospel; he shall tread down his enemies and crush them as grapes in the winepress. His shoes shall be iron and brass, and shod with them he shall stand upon the high places of the earth, and his feet shall not slip. Achilles received a deadly wound in the heel, but no arrow can pierce the heel of the man whose foot is sandalled with reconciliation by atoning blood. Many a warrior has fainted on the march and dropped from the ranks exhausted, but no weariness of the way can happen to the man who is upheld by the eternal God, for his strength shall daily be renewed.

The preparation of the gospel of peace must be understood to comprehend more than the legal peace of justification by faith. We must have the exceeding peace that springs from intimate, undisturbed communion with God. We should pray not only to feel that we have been brought out of our natural enmity into peace with God but also to dwell in the full joy of our new relationship as children. It is a sweet thing for a child of God to feel that he is so living that his heavenly Father has no reason for walking contrary to him. You know that as a child of God, you will not be condemned and cast away as an alien, but you also know that you may greatly displease your Father and render it needful for him to discipline you, and this you should with the utmost diligence and prayerfulness labor to prevent. There are times when the Lord of pilgrims hides His face from them in sore displeasure, and then it is very hard travelling. Life is "a great and terrible wilderness" when the Lord's presence is withdrawn. The more a man loves the Lord, the more he suffers when there is a temporary suspension of happy communion between his soul and heaven, and he cannot be happy again till he knows that he is fully restored to the Father's favor.

O child of God, you will very soon have your feet torn with the briers of the way if you do not abide in fellowship with God! When Adam lost his oneness with God, he discovered he was naked, and so will you if you lose your communion with Jesus. Where before you dashed onward as with a charmed life, treading the world and all its cares beneath your feet, you will find yourself pierced with many sorrows, bleeding with acute griefs, scratched, torn, lacerated with trials, losses, crosses, and annoyances endless. If we continue in the love of Jesus, pleasing Him in all things, jealously watching and carefully observing His will, our mind will be kept by the peace of God that passes all understanding, and our road to heaven will be a pleasant one. While it may indeed be very rough in itself and in the judgment of others, it will be so smoothed to us by the peace that reigns within that we shall glory in weakness, exult in suffering, and triumph in distress, knowing that the Lord is with us and no harm can come to us. Thus you see that the peace that comes from justification and the fuller peace that arises from enjoying the love of God are a grand preparation for our life's journey, a shoe for the foot unrivalled in excellence.

It is also a grand sandal for a pilgrim's foot when the gospel of peace has fully conformed the pilgrim's mind to the Lord's will. Some children of God are not at peace with God, because they do not fully acquiesce in the divine purposes. To them, the pilgrim path must be a painful one, for nothing can please them. Their unmortified self-will creates swarms of vexations for them, but to hearts that have crucified self and yielded all to the will of God, the most thorny paths are pleasant. He who can say concerning all things, "Even so, Father, for so it seemed good in thy sight," is prepared for all ways and weathers and may march on undismayed. Fully conformed to the divine will, saints are invulnerable and invincible, "none shall be weary nor stumble among them; . . . neither shall the . . . latchet of their shoes be broken" (Isa. 5:27).

Surely it is when the heart is completely at one with God that the true beauty of the Christian character is seen. Shod with perfect delight in the will of the Lord, we are able to surmount all the difficulties and trials of the way, for it becomes sweet to suffer when we see that it is the will of God. Resignation is good, but perfect acquiescence is better, and happy is the man who feels it. No silver sandals were ever so precious, no buskins of golden mail adorned with precious stones were so glorious to look upon as a mind molded to the divine will, perfectly in tune with the mind of the Lord Most High.

The preparation of the gospel of peace, as you can see, is, in many aspects, the fittest help for our journey to the Promised Land, and he who has his feet shod with it need not fear the flinty ways, the craggy rocks, or the thorny defiles.

But the gospel of peace has another side to it, for it not only brings us peace with God but also inspires us with *peace toward ourselves*. Civil war is the worst war, and for a man to be at discord with himself is the worst of strife. The worst peril of Christian pilgrimage is that which arises from the pilgrim's own self, and if the pilgrim is ill at ease within himself, his course cannot be a happy one. It is a cruel case for a man when his own heart condemns him. To whom shall he look for a defense when his own conscience indicts him and all his faculties turn king's evidence against him? It is to be feared that many believers habitually do things on which they would not like to be questioned by the rule of the Word of God. Such people have to close their eyes to many passages of Scripture or be uneasy in their consciences. This makes for wretched travelling. It is like walking through a woods with bare feet. If you cannot satisfy your own heart that you are right, you are in a sad case indeed, and the sooner matters are changed, the better.

But a man who proceeds with confidence can say before the living God, "I know that what I am about to do is right, and whatever comes of it, I have a pure motive and the Lord's sanction to sustain me in it." Such a pilgrim is prepared for roughest ways and will hold on his way joyfully to the end. Come what may, if we order our ways with reverent regard to the Lord's commands, we shall be able to confront the future with serenity, for we shall not have to accuse ourselves of bringing ourselves into trouble by sin or losing our joys by indulging in forbidden things. When the believer falls into any trouble through having been zealous for God, then may he spread his complaint before God with the full expectation that He will bring him out of all his difficulties, for it is written, "The steps of a good man are ordered by the LORD . . . none of his steps shall slide" (Ps. 37:23, 31). Oh, to walk in such a way that your conscience is void of offense both toward God and toward man—then integrity and uprightness will preserve you, and your goings will be established.

While travelling through the mazes of life, another form of the preparation of the gospel of peace will be of essential service to us—namely, *peace with our fellowmen*. The gospel of peace leads us into the closest bonds of amity with our fellow believers, although, alas, it is not always possible to prevent offenses arising, even with the best of them. If we cannot make all our brethren amiable, we are at least to be at peace on our side; and if we succeed in this, no great disagreement can arise, for it always requires two to make a quarrel. It is good to go to bed every night feeling, "I have no difference in my soul with any members of Christ's body; I wish all of them well and love them from my heart." This would enable us to travel royal style over fields that now are often stony with controversy and thorny with prejudice. Theological conflicts and squabbles would utterly disappear if we were shod with the true spirit of the gospel of peace. An unwillingness to think badly of any Christian is a sandal most easy to the foot, protecting it from many a thorn. Wear it in the church, wear it in all holy service, wear it in all fellowship with Christians, and you will find your way among the brethren greatly smoothed. You will before long win their love and esteem and avoid a world of jealousy and opposition that would otherwise have impeded your course.

It is best to travel with this shoe of *peace with all mankind*. "If it be possible, as much as lieth in you, live peaceably with all men" (Rom. 12:18). It is barely possible, but aim at it, and if you do not perfectly succeed, try again. You cannot help that the unconverted despise your religion, but you must love them, and by degrees you may win them to love both you and your Lord. If they will not live peaceably with you, yet give them your love and live peaceably with them. Be not easily provoked, bear and forbear, forgive and love on, return good for evil, seek to benefit even the most unthankful, and you will travel to heaven in the pleasantest manner. Hatred, envy, and persecution may come, but a loving spirit materially blunts their edge and oftentimes inherits the promise, "When a man's ways please the LORD, he maketh even his enemies to be at peace with him" (Prov. 16:7). If you set out to avenge a wrong, you will not journey pleasantly or safely; but if from the depth of your soul you can say, "When Christ made peace with God for me, he made peace between me and my bitterest foe," you will march on like a hero. God grant us that loving spirit that comes of free grace and is the work of the Holy Spirit, for it is a mystic sandal that gives wings to feet and lightens a weary load.

Having thus described these gospel shoes, I should like to say that the feet of our Lord and Master were sandalled in this manner. Jesus was the King of pilgrims, and to Him the way was even rougher than it can be to us; but these were the shoes He wore, and having worn them He counsels us to put on the same. "Peace I leave with you, my peace I give unto you" (John 14:27). He always walked in fellowship with God; He could truly say, "I came down from heaven, not to do mine own will, but the will of him that sent me. He that sent me is with me." Ever did He seek the good of His chosen: "having loved his own which were in the world, he loved them unto the end" (John 13:1). And as for His enemies, He had only prayers and tears for them; He was at peace with all above, around, and within Him. That peaceableness of His, that wonderful serenity, was one of the marvelous points of His character. You never find him worried, disturbed, flustered. No, that is *our* weakness, because we take our shoes off and are taken by surprise, but His feet were always shod. He dwelt in perfect peace, and therefore He was the grandest Pilgrim and the noblest Worker. We cannot be better shod than our Lord was. Let us sandal our hearts with His peace, and we shall be royally prepared for our journey.

I may add that these shoes are such as will last all our journey. We feel most comfortable in our old shoes, for they fit the foot so well, but they will wear out at last: these shoes of my text are old, yet ever new. The everlasting gospel yields us everlasting peace. The good news from heaven never grows stale. The man who wears the preparation of the gospel of peace was comforted by it when he was young, and it still cheers him in his later days. It made him a good traveller when he first set out, and it will protect his last footsteps when he crosses the river Jordan and climbs the celestial hills.

Let Us Try on These Shoes

Here our joy is great to find that *they fit perfectly* and need no tugging or straining to get them on. By a miracle more strange than magic, the preparation of the gospel of peace suits every foot, whether it be of a babe in grace or a strong man in Christ. No man can travel well, much less engage in battle successfully, unless his dress is comfortable, especially that part of it that relates to the feet, and here we have the grand advantage that no foot was ever uneasy once it put on this shoe. Mephibosheths who have been lame in both feet from their birth have found this shoe works miracles and causes them to leap as harts upon the mountains. The gospel of peace helps all our weaknesses, heals all the wounds of our old sins, and suits itself to all our tender places. Whatever the weakness may be, the gospel provides for it; whatever the distress, its peace relieves it. Other shoes have their pinching points, but he who wears the preparation of the gospel of peace shall know no straitness of spirit, for the gospel gives rest to our minds. Real gospel, really believed, means real peace. That which disturbs us is something alien to the spirit of the gospel, but the spirit of Christ is the spirit of peace. Who would not wear such a shoe?

The preparation of the gospel of peace is a wonderful shoe for *giving its wearer a firm foothold*. Surely it was of this shoe that Habakkuk sang, "The LORD God is my strength, and he will make my feet like hinds' feet, and he will make me to walk upon mine high places" (Hab. 3:19). When persons are on slippery rocks or dangerous cliffs where a fall would be fatal, it is essential to be so shod that the feet can grip and hold. Nothing aids a man to stand fast in the Lord like the peace of the gospel. Many believers are attacked with doctrinal error and yield easily; they are assailed by temptation, and out go their feet from under them. But the man who has peace with God and relies upon the Most High shall never be moved, for the Lord upholds him. His shoes have driven themselves into eternal certainties and hold like anchors. He knows whom he has believed and feels a heavenly peace within. Tell him that the doctrines of grace are a mistake, that salvation is all of free will and man's merit, and he says, "I know better. I know the doctrines of sovereign grace to be true by experience; I know that I have peace with God." You cannot move him an inch, his creed is interwoven with his personal consciousness, and there is no arguing him out of it. In these days of skepticism, it is good to be so shod that you can and do stand on the truth and cannot be blown about like thistledown in the breeze.

The shoe of our text is equally famous for its *suitability for marching* in the ways of daily duty. Soldiers have little time for considering the comfort of their shoes or their fitness for mere standing, for they have daily marchings to perform. We, too, have our marchings, heavy marches involving stern toil and protracted effort. A soul at perfect peace with God is in a fit state for the severest movements. A sense of pardoned sin and reconciliation with God fits us for anything and everything. When the burden of sin is gone, all other burdens are light. In every sphere, a heart at perfect peace with God is the soundest preparation for progress and the surest support under trials. Try on these shoes and see whether they do not enable you to run without weariness and walk without fainting. On earth they have no rival; they make men like the angels, to whom duty is delight.

These gospel shoes are also *an effectual preservative* from all the ordinary roughnesses of the road of life, although to most of us, the road is far from smooth. He who expects to find a grassy walk all the way to heaven will be sorrowfully mistaken. The way is rugged, like the goat tracks of Engedi, and oftentimes so narrow and so far on high that the eagle's eye cannot discern it. The blood of former pilgrims stains the way to glory, yet from all perils to our feet, the preparation of the gospel of peace will guard us; from fears within and fightings without, gospel peace will surely deliver us. Perhaps we are more vexed with little trials than with great ones. Certainly we bear them with far less equanimity, but a peaceful heart protects alike from tiny thorns and terrible rocks. Everyday vexations as well as extraordinary tribulations we shall bear cheerfully when the peace of God keeps our heart and mind.

This shoe is also *good for climbing*. Do you ever practice the holy art of spiritual climbing, God's blessed Spirit leading the way? Do you ever climb Mount Tabor to be transfigured with your Master? Have you watched with Him one hour and seen His conflict and victory? Have you ever looked from Pisgah's glorious heights upon the good land and Lebanon, anticipating the glory to be revealed? Has your spirit ever been away there alone in mysterious communings with God upon the Hermons? I trust you know what climbing work means and that you have enjoyed rapt ecstatic communings with Jesus Christ, but of this I am sure, you can never mount on high if your feet are not shod with the peace of God. Without these sacred sandals, there is no climbing. Only those who delight themselves in the Lord God shall ascend the hill of the Lord and stand in His holy place.

The heart prepared by peace with God is shod suitably for *running* as well as for climbing. There are periods when all our energies must be put forth and we must rush forward at the heroic pace, for at certain passages in life's campaign, things must be carried by storm and every faculty must dash forward at its swiftest speed. Troubled in heart, our foot is blistered, our knee is weak, and our movements are painfully slow; but the joy of the Lord is our strength, and in the power of it we become like Asahel, fleet of foot as a deer.

Lastly, this shoe is *good for fighting*, and that I gather from Paul having put it among the armor. In the old style, fighting meant hand to hand and foot to foot. Then it was needful for the feet to be well protected, and indeed so well covered over as to be useful in assault, for the warriors spurned with their feet as well as smote with their hands, and many a foe was brought down with a heavy kick. Christians are expected to fight with their feet in the battle against sin and Satan. Indeed, they must fight will all their powers and faculties. That grand promise has been given to us, "And the God of peace shall bruise Satan under your feet shortly" (Rom. 16:20). What a tread we will give him when we once have the opportunity! We shall need to have our feet shod with the preparation of the gospel of peace to break that old dragon's head and grind his snares to powder, and, God helping us, we shall do it. Our covenant Head has trampled on the old servant, and so shall all His members.

Let me also suggest that faith like a shield receives the blows that are meant for the believer. Some Christians think that faith should enable them to escape blows—that if they had faith, everything would be peaceful and calm. They think they are going to ride softly to heaven, singing all the way. Why do they put their armor on at all if they are to have no battles? Why enlist if you are not to fight? What good is a fair-weathered soldier who stays at home to feed at the public expense? No, let the soldier be ready when war comes; let him expect the conflict as a part and necessary consequence of his profession. But be armed with faith; it receives the blows. The poor shield is knocked and hammered and battered like a house exposed in a time of storm. Blow after blow comes rattling upon it, and though it turns death aside, yet the shield is compelled itself to hear the cut and the thrust. So must our faith do—it must be cut at, it must bear the blows.

Chapter Eleven

The Shield of Faith

Above all, taking the shield of faith, wherewith ye shall be able to quench all the fiery darts of the wicked—Ephesians 6:16.

LIKE THE SPARTANS, EVERY CHRISTIAN is born a warrior. It is his destiny to be assaulted, his duty to attack. Part of his life will be occupied with defensive warfare. He will have to defend the faith once delivered to the saints. He will have to resist the devil. He will have to stand against all the devil's wiles, and having done all, still to stand. He will, however, be an ineffective Christian if he acts only on the defensive. He must be one who goes against his foes as well as stands still to receive their advance. He must be able to say with David, "I come to thee in the name of the LORD of hosts, the God of the armies of Israel, whom thou hast defied" (1 Sam. 17:45). He must wrestle not with flesh and blood but against principalities and powers. He must have weapons for his warfare—not carnal—but "mighty through God to the pulling down of strong holds" (2 Cor. 10:4). He must not be content to live in the stronghold, though he is then well guarded and munitions of stupendous strength are at his disposal, but he must go forth to attack the castles of the enemy, pull them down, and drive the Canaanites out of the land.

There are many ways in which the Christian may to a great

degree forget his military character. And alas, there are many who know but very little of that daily warfare to which the Captain of our salvation calls His disciples! King David's truest soldiers were willing not only to be with David when he was in Saul's court with his fingers amid the strings of the harp, going in and out before the people so that "all Israel and Judah loved David" (1 Sam. 18:16), but also to go with David into the cave of Adullam when he was outlawed, when his character had become a stench in the nostrils of every proud hypocrite, and when Saul the king hunted David to seek his life. Those who are willing to follow Christ in the midst of an ungodly and perverse generation must be like the men of Naphtali, who hazarded their lives unto the death in the high places of the field.

You will remember that Jonathan, one of the sweetest characters in the Word of God, is one of whom after all there is little to be said. Jonathan's life was inglorious from the very time he forsook David, and his death was among the slain of the Philistines upon the dewless mountains of Gilboa. Alas, poor Jonathan, he could give David his bow, but he could not draw the bow for David; he could give David his garments, even his armor, but he could not put on the armor of David. The attraction of his father's court was too much for him, and there he stayed. In that Book of Chronicles, where the Holy Ghost has recorded the names of the mighty men who were with David in Adullam, we find not the name of Jonathan. There are Christians of that kind today. They have a soft religion that shuns opposition, a reedlike religion that bows before every blast, unlike that cedar of godliness that stands aloft in the midst of the storm and claps its boughs in the hurricane for the very joy of triumph. Such men, like those who shunned David in Adullam, lack the faith that shares the glory. Though saved, yet their names shall not be found written among the mighty men who for our Great Commander's sake are willing to suffer the loss of all things and to go forth without the camp bearing His reproach.

Those Christians, too, who have separated from the world and are diligently engaged in building up the church will have to fight more than others who are rather built up than builders. You remember, in Nehemiah's day, how the Jews accomplished their work when they built the walls of Jerusalem With one hand they held the trowel, and in the other they held a weapon. "The builders, every one had his sword girded by his side, and so builded" (Neh. 4:18). Moreover, there were master masons along the wall, and the laborers all actually engaged, yet here and there you might see a sentinel ready to sound the trumpet so that the workmen might prove warriors, rush to the battle, and drive away their foes. If you are diligent in your service to the church of Christ, you shall soon have reason to defend your cause. The Lord's blessing will entail Satan's curse; the smile of God will necessarily incur the frown of man. According to your nonconformity to the world, your daring to be singular—when to be singular is to be right—according to your diligence in building up the walls of Jerusalem, you shall be compelled to recognize your soldierly character. To you the text shall come with great emphasis, "Above all, take the shield of faith wherewith ye shall be able to quench all the fiery darts of the wicked."

Understanding the Metaphor

Faith is here compared to a shield. There are four or five particulars in which we may liken faith to a shield.

The natural idea that lies upon the very surface of the metaphor is that faith, like a shield, *protects us against attack*. The ancients used different kinds of shields, but there is a special reference in our text to the large shield that they sometimes employed. I believe the word that is translated "shield" sometimes signifies a door, because the ancients' shields were as large as a door. They covered the man entirely. You remember that verse in the Psalms that exactly hits the idea, "For thou, LORD, wilt bless the righteous; with favor wilt thou compass him as with a shield" (Ps. 5:12). As the shield enveloped the entire man, so faith envelops the entire man, protecting him from all missiles wherever they may be aimed against him. Faith protects the whole man. Let the assault of Satan be against the head, let Satan try to deceive us with unsettled notions in theology, let him tempt us to doubt those things that we have truly received. Unsettledness in our thoughts generally springs from a weakness of faith. A man who has strong faith in Christ has a hand that gets such a grip of the doctrines of grace that you could not unclasp it, do what you would. *He* knows what he has believed. *He* understands what he has received. *He* could not and would not give up what he knows to be the truth of God, though all the schemes that men devise should assail him with their most treacherous art.

While faith will guard the head, it will also guard the heart. When temptation to love the world comes in, faith holds up thoughts of the future and confidence of the reward that awaits the people of God and enables the Christian to esteem the reproach of Christ greater riches than all the treasures of Egypt, and so the heart is protected. Then when the enemy makes his cut at the sword arm of a Christian—to disable him, if possible, from future service—faith protects the arm like a shield, and the Christian is able to do exploits for his Master and go forth, still conquering and to conquer in the name of Him who loved us.

Suppose the arrow is aimed at the believer's feet and the enemy attempts to make him trip in his daily life—endeavors to mislead him in the uprightness of his walk and conversation. Faith protects the believer's feet, and the believer stands fast in slippery places. Neither does his foot slip, nor can the enemy triumph over him. Or suppose the arrow is aimed at the knee and Satan seeks to make him weak in prayer and tells him that God will not hear his cry. His faith protects him, and in the power of faith, with confidence, he has access to God and draws near to His mercy seat. Or let the arrow be aimed at the believer's conscience and let it be winged with the remembrance of some recent sin, yet faith protects the conscience, for its full assurance of atonement quenches the fiery darts with that delightful text: "The blood of Jesus Christ his Son cleanseth us from all sin" (1 John 1:7). So there is no part of a man that is not secure. Although Satan will certainly attack the believer in every direction, yet let him come where he will.

Not only does faith protect the whole man, but the Apostle Paul suggests that *faith also protects the man's armor*. After recounting various pieces, Paul says, "Above all." The man of God is to put on the belt and the breastplate, and he is to be shod, and he is to wear his helmet. But though these are all armor, yet faith is a defense for his defenses. Thus, faith shields not only the man but also the man's graces. You may easily perceive how this is. Satan sometimes attacks our sincerity; he tries to cut the belt of truth. But faith enables us to be fully sincere, like Moses who forsook Egypt, not fearing the wrath of the king, and refused to be called the son of Pharoah's daughter. Then the enemy will often make an attack against our righteousness, trying to batter our breastplate. Yet faith comes in and enables us like Joseph to exclaim, "How then can I do this great wickedness, and sin against God" (Gen. 39:9). Or like Job we cry, "Till I die I will not remove mine integrity from me" (Job 27:5).

You see how faith guards the breastplate and the belt. All our virtues are incomplete of themselves, they need grace to preserve them, and that grace is given us through faith. Are you meek? Cover your meekness with faith, or you will give way to a hasty speech. Are you full of determination? Let your decision be shielded with confidence in God, or your determination may waver and give way. Have you the spirit of love and gentleness? Take care that you have the shield of faith, or your gentleness may yet turn to anger and your love be changed to bitterness. All must be shielded by this all-covering, all-triumphant shield of faith.

Let me also suggest that faith like a shield *receives the blows that are meant for the man himself.* Some Christians think that faith should enable them to escape blows—that if they had faith, everything would be peaceful and calm. They think they are going to ride softly to heaven, singing all the way. Why do they put their armor on at all if they are to have no battles? Why enlist if you are not to fight? What good is a fair-weathered soldier who stays at home to feed at the public expense? No, let the soldier be ready when war comes; let him expect the conflict as a part and necessary consequence of his profession. But be armed with faith; it receives the blows. The poor shield is knocked and hammered and battered like a house exposed in a time of storm. Blow after blow comes rattling upon it, and though it turns death aside, yet the shield is compelled itself to hear the cut and the thrust. So must our faith do—it must be cut at, it must bear the blows.

Some people, instead of using the shield of faith to bear the blow, sneak away to the place of cowards. Ashamed of Christ, they make no profession of him, or having professed Christ, they hide themselves by conformity to the world. Perhaps they are even called to preach the gospel, but they do it in a quiet and gentle way. Unlike John the Baptist, they are "reeds shaken with the wind." No one speaks badly about them, because they do no damage to Satan's kingdom. Against them Satan never roars—why should he! "Let them alone," says he, "thousands such as these will never shake my kingdom."

Others use the shield of presumption, thinking all is well when it is not. Seared in their conscience as with a hot iron, they do not fear the rebukes of God's law. Deadened even to the voice of love, they will not bow before the invitations of Christ. They go on their way, caring for none of those things. Presumption has made them secure. Their shield lets them go through the world quietly, saying, "Peace, peace," where there is no peace. But only uplift the shield of faith, bearing the blood-red symbol of the cross, and there are plenty of knights of hell who are ready to unhorse you.

On champion, on, in the name of Him who is with you! No lance can pierce that shield; no sword shall ever be able to cut through it; it shall preserve you in all battle and strife; you shall bring it home yourself; through it, you shall be more than conqueror. Faith, then, is like a shield because it has to bear the blows.

Faith is also like a shield because it must be *strong*. A man who has some cardboard shield may lift it up against his foe; the sword will go through the shield and reach the enemy's heart. He who would use a shield must take care that it is a shield of strength. He who has true faith has such a shield that he will see the swords of his enemies go to a thousand shivers over it every time they strike. And if their spears but once come in contact with this shield, they will break into a thousand splinters or bend like reeds when pressed against the wall—they cannot pierce the shield but shall be quenched or broken in pieces.

You will say, how then are we to know whether our faith is a right faith? One test of it is, it must be a single piece. A shield that is made of three or four pieces in this case will be of no use. Your faith must be all of a piece; it must be faith in the finished work of Christ. You must have no confidence in yourself or in any other man but must rest wholly and entirely upon Christ, or your shield will be of no use. Then your faith must be of heaven's forging, or your shield will certainly fail you. Then you must see to it that your faith is that that rests only upon truth, for if there is any error or false notion in the fashioning of it, that will be a joint in it that the spear can pierce. You must take care that your faith is aligned to God's Word, that you depend upon true and real promises and not upon the fictions and dreams of men. And above all, you must mind that your faith is fixed in the person of Christ, for nothing but a faith in Christ's divine person and in His proper manhood when as the Lamb of God's passover He was sacrificed for us—no other faith will be able to stand against the tremendous shocks and the innumerable attacks that you must receive in the great battle of spiritual life.

To continue, faith is like a shield because it is of no use except it be *well handled*. A shield needs handling, and so does faith. He was a silly soldier who, when he went to battle, said he had a shield but it was at home. So there are some silly people who have a faith, but they have not got it with them when they need it. They have it with them when there are no enemies. When all goes well with them, then they can believe, but just when the pinch comes, their faith fails.

There is a sacred art in being able to handle the shield of faith. Let me explain to you how that can be. You handle it well if you are able to quote the *promises* of God against the attacks of your enemy. The devil said, "You will one day fall by the hand of the enemy." "No," said Faith, "for I am persuaded that He that began a good work in me will perform it until the day of Jesus Christ." "But," said Satan, as he shot another arrow, "you are weak." "Yes," said Faith, handling his shield, "but 'My strength is made perfect in weakness.' Most gladly therefore will I rather glory in my weaknesses, that the power of Christ may rest upon me." "But," said Satan, "your sin is great." "Yes," said Faith, handling the promise, "but he is able to save to the uttermost them who come unto God by him." "But," said the enemy again, drawing his sword and making a tremendous thrust, "God has cast you off." "No," said Faith. "He hates putting away; he does not cast off his people; neither does he forsake his heritage." "But I will have you, after all," said Satan. "No," said Faith, dashing the enemy's jaw. "He said, 'I give unto my sheep eternal life, and they shall never perish, neither shall any pluck them out of my hand.' " This is what I call handling the shield.

There is another way of handling it—not merely with the promises but with the *doctrines*. "What," asked Satan, "is there in you that you should be saved?" Up came Faith, handling the shield doctrinally this time, and said, "Hath not God chosen the poor of this world, rich in faith, and heirs of the kingdom that he hath promised to them who loved him?" "But," said he, "if God should have chosen you, yet after all you may certainly perish!" And then, the Christian, again handling his shield of faith doctrinally, said, "No, I believe in the final perseverance of the saints, for it is written, 'Those that thou gavest me I have kept, and none of them is lost.'" So by understanding the doctrines of grace, there is not a single doctrine that may not in its way minister to our defense against the fiery darts of the wicked.

Then, the Christian soldier ought to know how to handle the shield of faith according to the *rules of observation*. "But," says the enemy, "you have fallen into sin, and God will leave you." "No," says Faith, "for I saw David stumble, and yet the Lord surely brought him out of the horrible pit and out of the miry clay." To use this shield in the way of observation is very profitable when you mark how God has dealt with the rest of His people, for as He deals with one, so He will deal with the rest, and you can throw this in the face of your enemy: "I remember the ways of God. I call to remembrance His deeds of old. I say, has God cast off His people, has He forsaken one of His chosen? And since He has never done so, I hold up my shield with great courage and say He never will; He changes not; as He has not forsaken any, He will not forsake me."

Then there is another way of handling this shield, and that is *experientially*. When you can look back, like the Psalmist, to the land of Jordan and of the Hermonites, from the hill Mizar, when you can return to those days of old and call to remembrance your song in the night, when your spirit can say, "Why art thou cast down, O my soul? and why art thou disquieted within me? hope thou in God: for I shall yet praise him" (Ps. 42:11). Some of us can talk of so many deliverances that we know not where to end, scarcely do we know where to begin. Oh, what wonders has God done for us! He has brought us through fire and through water. His glory has appeared amidst all the villainies and slanders of men to which we have been exposed. Let us handle our shield, then, according to the rules of past experience, and when Satan tells us that God will fail us at the last, let us reply, "Now you lie, and I tell it to your face, for what our God was in the past, He will be in the present, and in the future, and even to the end." Young soldiers of Christ, learn well the art of handling your shield.

Lastly for the matter of the metaphor, the shield was *an emblem of the warrior's honor*, and more especially in later days than those of Paul. In the age of chivalry, the warrior carried his symbol upon his shield. Faith is like a shield because it carries the Christian's glory—the Christian's coat of arms. And what *is* the Christian's coat of arms? The Christian's best coat of arms is the cross of his Savior—that blood-red cross, always stained, yet never stained; always dyed in blood, yet always resplendent with ruby brightness; always trodden on, yet always triumphant; always despised, yet always glorified; always attacked, yet always without resistance, coming off more than conqueror. Put your coat of arms upon your shield and lift it up. Let that blood-red cross be your choice. Then when the battle is over, they will hang your shield up in heaven; and when the old heraldries have gone and the lions and the tigers and all manner of strange things have vanished from remembrance, that cross and your old dented shield shall be honorable with many a triumph before the throne of God. Above all things, then, take the shield of faith.

Enforcing the Exhortation

"Above all taking the shield of faith." If you sent a servant upon an errand and said to him, "Get this and that, but above all get such-and-such a thing," he would not understand that he should neglect any, but he would perceive that there was some extra importance attached to one part of his mission. So let it be with us. We are not to neglect our truthfulness, our righteousness, or our peace, but above all, as the most important, we are to see to it that our faith is right, that it is true faith, and that it covers all our virtues from attack.

The necessity of true faith is clearly explained by the text. The ancients were known to use small arrows—perhaps light cane arrows—that were tinged with poison. These arrows were called fiery darts because they no sooner touched the flesh or even grazed the skin than they left a fiery poison in the veins. Sometimes, too, the ancients employed darts that were tipped with material that had been dipped in some inflammable liquid and were blazing as they flew through the air in order to set the tents of their antagonists on fire or burn down houses in besieged cities. Now faith has a quenching power. It sees the temptation, or the blasphemy, or the insinuation that is coming against it with poison and with fire in it take away its life and burn up its comforts. Faith catches the dart; it not only receives it but also takes away its sting and quenches its fire.

It is wonderful how God sometimes enables His people to live in the midst of temptations and tribulations as though they had none of them. There are times when, though everyone speaks against us, our peace is like a river and our righteousness like the waves of the sea. Truly at such times we can say, "Now I am in my proper place; this is where I should be—outside the camp, bearing the reproach of Christ." The praise of man is deadly and damnable; man's censure is good and godlike. Let it come; it cannot dishonor, it does but ennoble. Thus does it often happen that faith quenches the fire of attack; nay, more, it turns the attack into comfort, extracts honey from the nettle and sweets of joy from the wormwood and the gall. "Above all, take the shield of faith."

Another commendation that the text gives is that faith alone, out of all the pieces of armor, is able to quench *all* the darts. The helmet can keep off only those darts that are aimed against the head. The foot is protected only by the sandals, and the breast alone is guarded by the breastplate, but faith protects against all attacks. Have all other virtues, but most of all, have faith, for faith is the cure-all. It is good for everything—good for the timid to make them strong, good for the rash to make them wise, good for those who are desponding to make them brave, and good for those who are too daring to make them discreet. There is no respect in which faith is not useful to us; therefore, whatever you leave out, see to your faith.

We are told above all to take the shield of faith *because faith preserves us from all sorts of enemies*. The fiery darts of the *wicked*? Does that refer to Satan? Faith answers him. Does it refer to wicked men? Faith resists them. Does it refer to one's own wicked self? Faith can overcome that. Does it refer to the whole world? "This is the victory that overcometh the world, even our faith" (1 John 5:4).

It matters not who the enemy is. Let the earth be all in arms abroad, this faith can quench all the fiery darts of the wicked. Above all, then, take the shield of faith. I know there are some who teach doubting as a duty. I cannot—I dare not. In the old Grecian contests, the aim of the enemy was to get near enough to push aside the shield and then to stab under the armor. That is what Satan wants to do. Take care of your shield. Do not live in perpetual unbelief. Be not always cast down. Pray to your God till you can say, "I know whom I have believed, and am persuaded that he is able to keep that which I have committed unto him" (2 Tim. 1:12). David said, "Say unto my soul, I am thy salvation" (Ps. 35:3). "The Lord is my light and my salvation" (Ps. 27:1). "The Lord is my shepherd" (Ps. 23:1). Job, too, could say, "I know that my redeemer liveth" (Job 19:25). Paul could speak in full confidence wherever he went. And why should we be content to say, "I hope, I trust," when they said they knew and were persuaded? Let it be so with us. Unbelief dishonors us, weakens us, destroys our comforts, prevents our usefulness. Faith will make us happy, make us useful, and enable us to honor God on earth and to enjoy His presence while yet we are in the lowlands of this present world.

A Word of Comfort

In John Bunyan's *Pilgrim's Progress*, Christiana and Mercy and the children come to knock at the gate. When they knocked, the enemy who lived in a nearby castle sent out a big dog that barked at them at such a rate that Mercy fainted and Christiana only dared to knock again, and when she obtained entrance, she was trembling. At the same time in the nearby castle, there were men who shot fiery darts at all who would enter, and poor Mercy was exceedingly afraid because of the darts and the dog. Whenever a soul comes to Christ, the devil will dog him. No matter what Satan brings against you, know that there is nothing that can bring joy and peace into your heart but faith. Satan fears your faith. Throw down the lies that only encumber and expose you, rendering you defenseless to his attacks. Take up the shield of faith.

For that shield of faith, say to Satan, "In the name of God I dare believe." "You are a great sinner," says he. "Yes, but I believe He is a great Savior." "But you have sinned beyond hope." "No, there is forgiveness with Him, that He may be feared." But he says, "You are shut out." "No," say you. "Though He slay me, yet will I trust Him." "But your disease is of long standing." But say you, "If I but touch the hem of His garment, I shall be clean." But says Satan again, "How dare you? Would you have the impudence?" "Well," say you, "if I perish, I will trust Christ, and I will perish only there." Have it in your soul fixed that whether Satan's accusations be true or false, you mean to fully answer them by simply trusting Christ Then you shall have such joy and peace that nothing shall be like it.

Oh, that you would believe in Jesus *now*! Leave your feelings, your doings, and your willings, and trust Christ. Say to God, "I have heart that You are merciful. If there is a wretch out of hell who deserves to be in it, I am that sinner—if there is one who now feels that the earth is provoked against him and the ground says, swallow him up, and heaven is provoked against him and cries, let the lightning flash destroy him, and the sea says, drown him, and the stars say, smite him with pestilence, and the sun says, scorch him, and the moon says, let him be blasted, and the mildew says, let me devour his crops, and fever says, let me cut off the thread of his life—if there be such a wretch out of hell, I am he." Yet say to God, "I believe in Your mercy, I believe in Your promise, I believe in Your Son Jesus, I believe in His precious blood, and here I am. Do with me as seems good in Your sight"—say this, and you shall have mercy, pardon, and peace.

*T*hrough long practice in sin, a man may have coated himself as with armor impenetrable, yet the Word of God will divide the best steel. The Holy Ghost can make a man feel the divine power of the sacred Word in the very center of his being. For battling with the spirits of man or with spirits of an infernal kind, there is no weapon so keen, so piercing, so able to divide between the joints and marrow, so penetrating as to the thoughts and intents of the heart. The Word in the Spirit's hand gives no flesh wound but cuts into the man's heart so deeply that there is no healing save by supernatural power. The wounded conscience will bleed. Its pains will be upon it day and night, and though it seek a thousand medicines, no salve but one can cure a gash that this terrible sword has made. This weapon is two-edged. Indeed, it is all edge, and whichever way it strikes, it wounds and kills. He who uses the Word in the Lord's battles may use it upon carnal hopes and then strike back upon unbelieving fears. He may smite with one edge the love of sin and then with the other the pride of self-righteousness. It is a conquering weapon in all ways, this wondrous sword of the Spirit of God.

Chapter Twelve

The Sword of the Spirit

And take . . . the sword of the Spirit, which is the word of God
—Ephesians 6:17.

TO BE A CHRISTIAN IS TO BE A WARRIOR. The good soldier of Jesus Christ must not expect to find ease in this world, for the world is a battlefield, and the Christian's occupation is war. As he puts on piece by piece of the armor provided, the believer may wisely say to himself, "This warns me of danger; this prepares me for warfare; this prophesies opposition."

Difficulties meet us even in standing our ground, and the Apostle Paul, two or three times, commands us: "Stand." In the rush of the fight, men are apt to be knocked down. If they can keep their footing, they will be victorious; but if they are borne down by the rush of their adversaries, everything is lost. You are to put on the heavenly armor so that you may stand, and you will need it to maintain the position in which your Captain has placed you. If simply to stand requires all this care, consider what the warfare must be! The apostle also speaks of *withstanding* as well as standing. We are not merely to defend but also to assail. It is not enough that we are not conquered; we have to conquer, and hence we find that we are to take a sword with which to fight. Ours, therefore, is a stern conflict, standing and withstanding, and we shall need all the armor from the divine Captain, all the strength from the mighty God of Jacob.

It is clear from the text that our defense and conquest must be obtained by sheer fighting. Many try compromise, but if you are a true Christian, you can never do this business well. The language of deceit does not fit a holy tongue. The adversary is the father of lies, and those who are with him understand the art of equivocation, but saints abhor it. We have no order from our Captain to patch up a truce or offer concessions. It is said that if we yield a little, perhaps the world will yield a little also, and good may come of it. No such thing. Neither may we hope to gain by being neutral and as agreeable as we can with our Lord's foes, participating in their pleasures and tasting their dainties. No such orders are written here. You are to grasp your weapon and go forth to fight.

Neither may you dream of winning the battle by accident. No man was ever holy by random chance. Infinite damage may be done by carelessness, but no man ever won life's battle by it. To let things go on as they please is to let them carry us down to hell. We have orders instead to pray always and watch constantly. The one note that rings out is this: TAKE THE SWORD! TAKE THE SWORD! No longer is it talk and debate and compromise! The word of thunder is, *Take the sword!* The Captain's voice is clear as a trumpet. No Christian will have been obedient to the text unless with clear, sharp, and decisive firmness, courage, and resolve he takes the sword. We must go to heaven sword in hand, all the way.

It is noteworthy that there is only one weapon of offense provided, although there are several pieces of armor. The Roman soldier usually carried a spear as well as a sword. But Paul, for excellent reasons, concentrates our offensive weapon in one, because it answers for all. We are to use *the sword*, and that only. If you are to have no other, take care that you have this always in your hand. Let the Captain's voice ring in your ear, "*Take the sword!*," and so go forth to the field.

The Sword You Are to Take

The Word of God that is to be our one weapon is of noble origin: "the sword of the Spirit." It has the properties of a sword, and those were given to it by the Spirit of God.

Here we note that *the Holy Spirit has a sword.* He is quiet as the dew, tender as the anointing oil, soft as the breeze of evening, and peaceful as a dove; and yet, He wields a deadly weapon. He is the Spirit of judgment and the Spirit of burning, and He bears not the sword in vain. Of Him it may be said, "The Lord is a man of war: Jehovah is his name."

The Word of God in the hand of the Spirit wounds very terribly and makes the heart of man to bleed. Were you not cut to the heart by it, so as to be angry with it? Perhaps you almost made up your mind to turn away from the gospel. That sword pursued you and pierced you in the secrets of your soul, making you bleed in a thousand places. At last you were "pricked in the heart," which is a far better thing than being "cut to the heart"; and then the execution was done. That wound was deadly, and none but He that killed could make you alive. Do you recall how, after this, your sins were slain one after another? Their necks were laid on the block, and the Spirit acted as an executioner with His sword. After that—blessed be God—your fears, doubts, despair, and unbelief were also hacked to pieces by this same sword. The Word gave you life, but it was first a great killer. Your soul was like a battlefield after a great fight, under the first operations of the divine Spirit whose sword returns not empty from the conflict.

Make no mistake, the Spirit of God is at war with the Amalek of evil and error from generation to generation. He will spare none of the evils that now pollute the nations; His sword will never be quiet till all these Canaanites are destroyed. The Holy Spirit glorifies Christ not only by what He reveals but also by what He overturns. The strife may be weary, but it will be carried on from age to age till the Lord Jesus shall appear. Forever shall the Spirit of God espouse the cause of love against hate, of truth against error, of holiness against sin, of Christ against Satan. He will win the day, and those who are with Him shall in His might be more than conquerors. The Holy Spirit has proclaimed war and wields a two-edged sword.

The Holy Spirit wields no sword but the Word of God. This wonderful Book, which contains the utterances of God's mouth, is the one weapon that the Holy Ghost elects to use for His warlike purposes. It is a spiritual weapon and so is suitable for the Holy

Spirit. The weapons of His warfare are not carnal. He never uses persecution or patronage, force or bribery, glitter of grandeur or terror of power. He works upon men by the Word, which is suitable to His own spiritual nature and to the spiritual work that is to be accomplished. Although it is spiritual, this weapon is "mighty through God." A cut from the Word of God will cleave a man's spirit from head to foot, so sharp is this sword.

Through long practice in sin, a man may have coated himself as with armor impenetrable, yet the Word of God will divide the best steel. The Holy Ghost can make a man feel the divine power of the sacred Word in the very center of his being. For battling with the spirits of man or with spirits of an infernal kind, there is no weapon so keen, so piercing, so able to divide between the joints and marrow, so penetrating as to the thoughts and intents of the heart. The Word in the Spirit's hand gives no flesh wound but cuts into the man's heart so deeply that there is no healing save by supernatural power. The wounded conscience will bleed. Its pains will be upon it day and night, and though it seek a thousand medicines, no salve but one can cure a gash that this terrible sword has made. This weapon is two-edged. Indeed, it is all edge, and whichever way it strikes, it wounds and kills. He who uses the Word in the Lord's battles may use it upon carnal hopes and then strike back upon unbelieving fears. He may smite with one edge the love of sin and then with the other the pride of self-righteousness. It is a conquering weapon in all ways, this wondrous sword of the Spirit of God.

The Word is the only sword that the Spirit uses. I know the Holy Ghost uses gracious sermons, but only in proportion to how much of the Word of God is in them. I know the Holy Ghost uses books but only so far as they are the Word of God told in another language. Conviction, conversion, and consolation still are wrought only by the Word of God. Learn, then, the wisdom of using the Word of God for holy purposes. The Spirit has abundant ability to speak of His own self apart from the written Word.

The Holy Ghost is God, and therefore He is is the greatest spirit in the universe. All wisdom dwells in Him. He thought out the laws that govern nature and direct providence. The Holy Spirit is the great teacher of human spirits: He taught Bezaleel and the artificers in the wilderness how to make the fine linen and the gold and carved work for the tabernacle. All arts and sciences are perfectly known to Him and infinitely more than men can ever discover. Yet in the quarrel of His covenant, He uses neither philosophy nor science nor rhetoric. In contending against the powers of darkness, "The sword of the Spirit is the word of God." "It is written" is the Spirit's master stroke. Words that God has spoken by holy men of old and has caused to be recorded on the sacred page—these are the battle-ax and weapons of war of His Spirit. This Book contains the Word of God, and is the Word of God; and this it is that the Holy Ghost judges to be so effectual a weapon against evil that He uses this, and this only, as His sword in the great conflict with the powers of darkness.

The Word is the sword of the Spirit because it is of the Spirit's own making. The Holy Spirit will not use a weapon of human workmanship lest the sword boast itself against the hand that wields it. The Holy Ghost revealed the mind of God to the minds of holy men. He spoke the word into their hearts and thus made them think as He would have them think and to write what He willed them to write, so that what they spoke and wrote was spoken and written as they were moved by the Holy Ghost. Blessed be the Holy Spirit for choosing to use so many writers and yet Himself to remain the veritable Author of this collection of holy books. We are grateful for every contributor, but most of all for that superintending Editor, that innermost Author of the whole sacred volume.

A warrior is careful as to the quality and make of his sword. If a man had made his own sword, had tempered the metal, had passed the blade through many fires and worked it to perfection, then, if he were a skillful workman, he would feel confidence in his sword. The Holy Ghost has made this Book Himself: every portion of it bears His initial and impress, and thus He has a sword worthy of His own hand, a true Jerusalem blade of heavenly quality. He delights to use a weapon so divinely made, and He does use it gloriously.

The Word of God is also the sword of the Spirit because the Spirit puts the edge upon it. It is because the Spirit is in it that the sword is so keen and cutting. I believe in the inspiration of the Holy Scripture, not only in the day when it was written but onward, and even to this day. The Word is still inspired; the Holy Ghost still breathes through the chosen words. I told you the sword was all edge, but

I would add that the Holy Spirit makes it so. The sword would have no edge at all if it were not for the Spirit's presence within it and His perpetual working by it. How many people read their Bibles and yet derive no more benefit from it than if they had read a newspaper. The ministers of the gospel may preach God's Word in all sincerity and purity, and yet, if the Spirit of God is not present, we might as well have preached moral essays. The Holy Ghost rides in the chariot of Scripture and not in the wagon of modern thought. Scripture is that ark of the covenant that contains the golden pot of manna and bears above it the divine light of God's shining. The Spirit of God works in, by, through, and with the Word, and if we keep to that Word, we may rest assured that the Holy Ghost will keep with us and make our testimony to be a thing of power. Let us pray the blessed Spirit to put an edge on our witness, lest we say much and accomplish little.

It is "the sword of the Spirit" because *the Holy Spirit alone can instruct us in the use of it.* A sword is a weapon that can hurt the person who is untrained in handling it. And no one can properly handle the sword of the Spirit except those trained in the feats of arms. By this the elect of God are known—that they love the Word of God and discern between it and the words of men. Notice the lambs in a field of a thousand ewes and lambs, but every lamb finds its own mother. So does a child of God know where to go for the milk that is to nourish his soul. The sheep of Christ know the Shepherd's voice in the Word, and a stranger they will not follow. God's own people have discernment to discover and relish God's own Word. They will not be misled by the cunning craftiness of human devices. Saints know the Scriptures by inner instinct. The holy life, which God has infused into believers by His Spirit, loves the Scriptures and learns how to use them for holy purposes.

Young soldier, you must go to the training ground of the Holy Spirit to be made an expert swordsman. The Holy Spirit must take the things of Christ and show them to us. He must teach us how to grip this sword by faith and how to hold it by watchfulness so as to parry the adversary's thrust and carry the war into the foe's territory. He is well taught who can swing this great two-edged sword to and fro, mowing a lane through the midst of his opponents and conquering to the end. It may take a long time to learn this art, but we have a skillful Teacher. Those of us who have been in this warfare thirty or forty years feel that we have not yet reached the full use of this sword. I know that I need daily to be taught how to use this mysterious weapon, which is capable of so much more than I have yet supposed. It is the sword of the Spirit, adapted for the use of an Almighty arm and therefore equal to the doing of far more than we think. Holy Spirit, teach us new feats of arms by this Your sword!

Chiefly, it is the sword of the Spirit because *He is the great Master in the use of it.* Oh, that He would come and show us how He can thrust and cleave with it! By this sword He has taken off the head of many a Goliath doubt and slain a horde of cares and unbeliefs. The Spirit piles up heaps on heaps of the slain when the Word of conviction goes forth, and men have seen sin to be sin and fallen down as dead before the Lord and His law. It is by the sword of the Spirit that God has left marks of His power within our inner being. The great giant of doubt is sorely wounded by the sword of the Spirit—yea, he is slain outright, for the Spirit works in the believer such a conviction of the truth that assurance banishes suspicion. When the Holy Spirit deals with the lusts of the flesh, the lusts of the eye, and the pride of life, these also lie at His feet, trophies to the power of His mighty weapons, even the Word of God! The Holy Spirit is glorious in the use of this sword. He finds that this weapon suits His hand, and He seeks no other. Let us use it also and be glad to do so. Though it is the sword of the Spirit, yet our feebler hand may grasp it and find in the grasping that something of the divine power comes into our arm.

Is it not a very high honor that soldiers of the cross are commanded to take the sword of the Spirit? The new recruit is not trusted with the general's sword, but here you are armed with the Holy Spirit's weapon and called upon to bear that sacred sword that is so gloriously wielded by the Lord God Himself. Does the timid heart ask, "How shall I meet my adversaries?" "Here," says the Holy Ghost, "take this! This is my own sword; I have done great marvels with it. Take it, and nothing shall stand against you." When you remember the potency of this sword, when the Spirit tests it upon yourself, you may take it with confidence and use it in your holy war with full assurance. That Word of God that converted *you* can convert anybody. If it could kill your despair, it can remove another's despondency. If it has conquered your pride and self-will, it can subdue the same in your children and neighbors. Having done what it has for you, you may be fully persuaded that before its power no case is hopeless. See to it that you use no other weapon than the sword of the Spirit, which is the Word of God.

This Sword Is to Be Ours

Our warfare is not child's play: *we shall need a sword*. We have to deal with fierce foes who are to be met only with the best weapons. You may be of a very quiet spirit, but your adversaries are not. If you attempt to play at Christian warfare, they will not. To meet the powers of darkness is no pretend battle. Nothing but your eternal damnation will satisfy the fiendish hearts of Satan and his crew. In this combat, you will have to use a sword such as even evil spirits can feel. If you are to live through this fight and come away victorious, you will be forced to fight at close quarters. The foe aims at the heart and pushes home. A spear will not do, nor bow and arrow. The enemy is too near for anything but hand-to-hand fighting. And our foes are not only of our house but also of our heart. I find an enemy within that is always near, and I cannot get away from him. Now for the short sword of Holy Scripture, to stab and cut, near and now. No sling and stone will avail us here, but we must take the sword. You have to slay your foe, or your foe will slay you.

The use of the sword is needful for attack. It will not suffice for the Christian to guard against sin and ward off tempting; he has to assail the powers of evil. In our case, the best method of defense is an attack. Carry the warfare into the enemy's territory. Do not merely be sober yourself, but attack drunkenness. Do not be content with being free from lies, but expose them wherever they appear. Do not merely be devout, but pray for the growth of the kingdom—pray always. Do not merely say, "I will keep Satan out of my family by bringing up my children correctly," but take your children to Sunday school and teach other children, and so carry the war over the border. If we had fought the devil more in the world, he might never have been able to invade the church so terribly as he has done. Attack with the sword, for it is your calling, and thus will you best defend yourself.

We need the sword for real fighting. Do you think you can dream yourself into heaven or ride there in the chariot of ease or fly on the wings of brass music? You make a great mistake if you imagine you can. A real war is raging, your opponents are in deadly earnest, and you must take *this sword, the Word of God*. The sword has wrought such wonders that we prefer it to all others. No other will match the enemy's weapon. If we fight the devil with human reason, the first time our wooden sword comes in contact with a satanic temptation it will be cut in pieces. If you do not wield a true Jerusalem blade, you are in grave peril. Your weapon will break off at the hilt, and where will you be? Standing defenseless, with nothing but the handle of a broken sword in your hand, you will be the object of your adversary's ridicule. You must have *this* sword, for no other will penetrate the foe, and no other will last throughout the battle. The Word of the Lord endures forever, but nothing else does. Our consecration may serve us well in early days, but we shall fail in old age if we have not eternal truths to fall back on.

I can commend this sword as one that fits every hand. Young and old can use this weapon. Boys and girls leave the Bible class to fight the battle of their youth with the Word of God, for Holy Scripture may impress and guide the most youthful life. You who have grown gray will value the Bible more than ever, and you will find that this sword is the best for veteran warriors. Here is a sword suited for all, and well does it strengthen the hand of the feeblest and gentlest. The Holy Ghost has in the sacred Word prepared an implement of warfare suited for great minds and small, for the cultured and the uneducated. A wonderful sword this is, which in the hand of faith reveals an adaptation marvelous to the highest degree.

We are told *to take this sword*. Note that we are not told that we may lay it down. The command to take the sword is continuous, and there is no hint of its being suspended. There is a time, of course, when the soldier may remove his sword and put off his armor. There is never such a time with a Christian. One might have thought from what we have seen lately that orders had come from headquarters to lay down the Word of God and take to lighter weapons. Entertainments and amusements are now used to do what the gospel has failed to achieve. Is it not sadly so? If any will try these silly toys, I can only say that they have no authority from their Lord to warrant their use.

The standing orders are to take the sword of the Spirit. All other things will surely fail. We are not told to hang up this sword for exhibition. Certain people have a handsomely bound Bible to lie upon the table of the best room—and a fine ornament it is. But do not let your love of the Bible end there. With a soldier in war, a sword is not meant to be hung up in the tent but is issued to be used. Nor are we to push this sword into a sheath, as many do who take the Bible and add so much criticism or their own opinion to it that its edge is not felt. Their vast knowledge makes a beautiful scabbard, and they push down the sword, saying, "Keep still there! O sword of the Lord, rest and be quiet!" After we have preached our heart out and men have felt the power of it, they make a desperate effort to imprison the Word in their unbelieving theory or in their worldliness. They hold down the Word with a firm hand for fear its edge or point should wound them. It is the scabbard of culture or philosophy or progress, and in this they shut up the living Word of God as in a coffin.

We are not to bury the Word under other matters, but we are to take it as a sword, which means, as I understand it, first, *believe it*. Believe every portion of it. Believe it with a true and real faith. Believe it as a matter of fact for every day, affecting your life. And when you have believed it, then *study it*. Oh, for a closer study of the Word of God! Perhaps you have never even read all that the Lord has said. You need to read the Bible straight through, from beginning to end. Begin today and go steadily through the whole of the sacred book, with prayer and meditation. Let it never be said that God has recorded truths in His Word that you have not read. Study the Word and work out its meaning. Go deep into the spirit of inspiration. He gets the most gold who digs the deepest in this mine. The deeper you go under the Spirit's guidance, the larger the reward for your toil.

Take the sword with the grip of sincere faith, hold it fast by a fuller knowledge, and then exercise yourself daily in its use. It will not be long before occasion arises in such a world as this. You will have to parry with it, pierce with it, cut with it, and kill with it. Begin at home, and for many days you will have your hands full. When you have slain all the rebels at home—and long before that—you may take a turn at those around you in the world. Inside your own heart you will find a band of bandits that should be exterminated. There will always be a need to keep the sword going within your own territory. End this civil war before you go into foreign parts. When the war within the city of Mansoul has been victoriously carried through, besiege the heart of your friend, your child, your neighbor. Behold, the world lies in the power of the wicked one! Errors abound, and colossal systems of falsehood still stand aloft. Men are still dragged down by the arch-deceiver. Surely we feel our swords flying out of their sheaths when we think of the millions who are being ruined by sin and error. Oh, for a mighty onslaught upon the powers of darkness!

We are to take this sword that we may be able to stand and to withstand. If you want to stand, draw the sword and smite your doubts. How fiercely unbelief assails! Here comes a doubt about your election. Pierce it through with the Word. Then comes a doubt as to the precious blood. Cleave it from head to foot with the assurance of the Word that the blood of Jesus cleanses us from all sin. Here comes another doubt, and yet another. As quickly as your arm can move, drive texts of Scripture through every new fallacy, every new denial of truth, and split the whole of them upon the rapier of the Word.

You will find that temptations also will come in hordes. Meet them with the precepts of Scripture and slay even the desire of evil by the Spirit's application of the Holy Word. The washing of the water by the Word is a glorious cleanser. Discouragements will arise like mists of the morning. Oh, that God's Word may shine them away with the beams of the promises! Your afflictions multiply, and you will never be able to overcome impatience and distrust except by the infallible Word of God. You can withstand trials and bear them patiently if you use the weapon to kill anxiety. You will "stand fast in the evil day," and having done all, you still stand if this sword is in your hand.

You not only have to stand fast yourselves but also have to win souls for Christ. Do not try to conquer sin in others or capture a heart for Jesus except with the sword of the Spirit. How the devil laughs when we try to make converts apart from Holy Scripture and the Holy Spirit! He laughs, for he derides our folly. What can you do against men covered from head to foot with the steel armor of the habit of sin? Sunday-school teachers, teach your children more and more the pure Word of God. And preachers, do not try to be original but be content to take the things of Christ and declare them to the people, for that is what the Holy Ghost does, and you will be wise to use His method and His sword. No sinner will be saved except by the knowledge of the great truths contained in the Word of God. No one will ever be brought to repentance, to faith, and to life in Christ apart from the constant application of the truth through the Spirit. I hear great shouting, great noises everywhere, about great things that are going to be done: let us see them. If the champion goes forth with any other sword than the Word of God, he had better not boast at all, for he will come back with his sword broken, his shield cast away, and himself grimy with dishonor. Defeat awaits that man who forsakes the Word of the Lord.

Remember the text is in the present tense: *take the sword of the Spirit even now.* Believers find themselves in all sorts of perils. Let them take the sword of the Spirit and they will overcome every foe. "Oh," says one, "I have been in the habit of sinning, and the habit is very strong upon me." Fight sinful habits with the Word of God: conquer your evil self. Find a text of Scripture that will stab your sin in the heart. "Alas, Satan tempts me horribly!" says another. Does he? Are you the first? Our divine Lord in the wilderness was tempted by the devil. He might have fought Satan with a thousand weapons, but He chose to defeat him with this weapon only: "It is written." He pricked the enemy so sorely with this sharp point that the arch-adversary thought to try the same sword, and he also began to say, "It is written." But he cut himself with this sword, for he did not quote the passages correctly, and the Master soon found the way to knock aside his sword and wound him still more.

Follow your Lord's example. Someone says, "But I am depressed." Very well. Fight depression with the Word of God. I find that if I can lay a promise under my tongue, like a sweet lozenge, and keep it in my mouth or mind all day long, I am happy enough. If I cannot find a Scripture to comfort me, my inward troubles are multiplied. Fight despondency and despair with the sword of the Spirit. I do not know what your particular difficulty may be at this moment, but I give you this direction for all holy warfare: "Take the sword of the Spirit, which is the word of God." You must overcome every enemy, and this weapon is all you need.